Quantum Economics and Abundant Wealth: Overcoming the

Paradoxical and the Satanic

Atticus Clemens

2016

Table of Contents

I.   Introduction

In March 2004 I lost a dear family member to Lung Cancer. At the memorial service a family friend had just read Dan Brown's newly published *Da Vinci Code*. She shared with me the premise of the book. I was mesmerized by these ideas, I could not wait to read it.   On the flight home from New York to California I read most of the book finishing it within a few days after arriving home. I could not put it down. I never suspected that Christ's story could have included marriage and potentially children. Further, after considering the possible validity of these unexpected ideas I was compelled to study all aspects of the circumstances that I could obtain.

This experience took me through an investigation of human history: from early Egyptian history and the mystery of the pyramids, through Greece and Rome, to First Century Judea, the fall of Rome and the Rise of the Roman Catholic Church in Western Europe. The Arthurian and Grail Legends, as they may extend back to their first century Christian roots in the British Isles along with the Magdalene legends of Southern France were of keen interest for their possible historic implications and the truths that might be revealed through their study.

Arrived at this point, the events of Western Europe leading up to the Crusades and Inquisition era were likewise of keen importance. When learning for the first time that a Crusade was in fact waged on the soil of Western Europe against what the Catholic Church deemed the Cathar Heretics of the Languedoc region of Southern France I was greatly surprised if not stunned by this unexpected fact.

As I continued, the legends surrounding the Templar Knights and their curious rise to power in a short time was irresistible to my curiosity. Their rise to power seemed to spring from banking services developed to facilitate Christian pilgrimage from the West to the Holy Land. While certainly a necessary and potentially lucrative business enterprise it, based upon my 20 years of experience as an institutional financial and economic analysts seemed insufficient to explain the extent of their quick rise to power. What was the Templar's function? In addition to securing safe travel along pilgrimage routes Templar legend includes their excavation of the Temple

Mount, the site of Solomon's Temple. Did they find something of great value? If so what did they find? The imagery of the Holy Grail as well as the Philosophers' Stone came to mind.

This led me to the Alchemists. Their ostensive quest to turn base metals to gold. Many great minds of the pre-scientific era up to and including Sir Isaac Newton were Alchemists. Were they really attempting to turn base metals to gold? Or were they on a quest that was an allegorical permutation of the transformative nature of Alchemy?

The possibilities opened to my mind through the premise of *The Da Vinci Code* brought me through a journey to a specific destination. That destination was the miraculous transformations of the Alchemists and the prospects of eternal life through the Holy Grail. To a certainty I have found the mechanisms of both miraculous transformation and eternal life through the Holy Grail. It is the purpose of this work to attempt to share these findings and in so doing contribute to the emergence of the *New Jerusalem* as prophesied:

> *Then I saw "a new heaven and a new earth," for the first*
>
> *heaven and the first earth had passed away, and there was*

no longer any sea. I saw the Holy City, the new Jerusalem, coming down out of heaven from God, prepared as a bride beautifully dressed for her husband. And I heard a loud voice from the throne saying, "Look! God's dwelling place is now among the people, and he will dwell with them. They will be his people, and God himself will be with them and be their God. 'He will wipe every tear from their eyes. There will be no more death' or mourning or crying or pain, for the old order of things has passed away."

Revelation 21: 1- 4

As to miraculous transformation, my great teacher was the literature and more importantly the members of *Alcoholics Anonymous*. Within two days of returning home from New York I recognized for the first time that I had a problem with alcohol. In that instant I went from believing that I had no problem with drinking, to an impossible problem for which I had no vision of a solution. I had a sincere and urgent desire to stop drinking yet I was compelled against the most powerful desire to not drink, to drink. Upon this discovery I slipped into a freefall of panic and anxiety. I intuitively knew that if I did not stop drinking horrific events would befall the people who I loved and cherished most yet I could not stop. On the morning of March 12 as I was outgassing the toxins of the previous night's quarts of scotch my mind raced uncontrollably toward a solution for this seemingly impossible problem, "I must stop drinking and I cannot", what to do? As I reflected upon this I framed the question in my mind "what do people with alcoholic problems do?" The answer to the cogently framed question came quickly. "They go to AA." So I called for the location and time and I went.

At the first meeting I attended at 5.30 PDT March 12, 2004, I saw people at the meeting who were happy. Moreover their happiness was noticeably genuine in a way that was somehow distinguishable from happiness I had previously known. During the meeting three gentlemen shared their experience, strength and hope as it related to their alcoholism. In clear and specific terms that I have come to recognize as the *"language of the heart"*, they shared how they drank before they got sober. *They each drank just as I did.* They then shared the deep despair that their drinking had brought them to. *That was the precise despair and anxiety I felt with intensity at that moment.* Finally, they shared that they did several things on a regular basis and in particular they worked the 12 steps of recovery and that as they started that process they were relieved of the uncontrollable urge to drink. From my perspective at that moment of intense fear, hopelessness and despair, those words spoken in the *"language of the heart"* reached to me as a genuine lifeline pulling me back from the edge of destruction. As that meeting progressed I read the text of the 12 Steps which were posted on the wall. I found it very curious that the text of the 12 steps mentioned very little about alcoholism yet discussed God and a power greater than oneself often. This was curious yet from my perspective, the connection between God and my problematic drinking at that moment made clear sense, it was plausible.

The principal author of the big book of Alcoholics Anonymous was a Wall Street analysts. A similar vocation to my own. As I read the text I could feel a connection with the author's thought process. It mirrored my own. His process of growing his belief and certainty in the truth of a Higher Power's role in the recovery from chronic alcoholism was a path I could jump on and follow. His manner of presenting evidence and analysis to support assertions I found convincing. In particular, consider the following excerpt:

A certain American businessman had ability, good sense, and high character. For years he had floundered from one sanitarium to another. He had consulted the best known American psychiatrists. Then he had gone to Europe, placing himself in the care of a celebrated physician (the psychiatrist, Dr. Jung)... ... The doctor [Jung} said: "You have the mind of a chronic alcoholic. I have never seen one single case recover, where that state of mind existed to the extent that it does in you." Our friend felt as though the gates of hell had closed on him with a clang.

He said to the doctor, "Is there no exception?"

"Yes," replied the doctor, "there is. Exceptions to cases such as yours have been occurring since early times. Here and there, once in a while, alcoholics have had what are called vital spiritual experiences. To me these occurrences are phenomena. They appear to be in the nature of huge emotional displacements and rearrangements. Ideas,

14

emotions, and attitudes which were once the guiding forces

of the lives of these men are suddenly cast to one side, and

a completely new set of conceptions and motives begin to

dominate them.

Alcoholics Anonymous (2001), pp. 26-27

The preceding excerpt is one of the most compelling passages in the text, perhaps the most compelling from my perspective. The validity of the observation from my perspective approaches a certainty through its source *CG Jung*. In retrospect I recognize that I had the mind of the chronic alcoholic Jung refers to. That in his opinion, chronic alcoholics NEVER recover. With the following exception: *"that here and there, once in a while alcoholics have vital spiritual experiences, to me these occurrences are phenomena, they appear to be in the nature of huge emotional displacements and rearrangements. Ideas, emotions and attitudes which were once the guiding forces of the lives of these men are suddenly cast to one side, and a completely new set of conceptions and motives begin to dominate them".*

I have come to see and know that the 12 steps are algorithmic in their nature. The process of the steps results in a radical and rapid reorientation of the consciousness of any person who undertakes to work them. That the state of consciousness a chronic alcoholic is in is fundamentally insane, or stated alternatively built upon a false root assumption of truth. That false assumption is the nature of self as a disconnected entity from the balance of the universe, or stated alternatively disconnected from A Power Greater Than himself or God. There is no such disconnection. The spiritual experience referred to by Jung is the process of the opening one's eyes to the true nature of the universe's interconnectivity and the individual as an integrated element of that unified field. An individual or self is not a fully contained entity, it is as we shall see later in this work, is a specific manifestation of the oneness of the universe, a Power Greater than Oneself, or if you prefer, God.

The miraculous is real and not imagined. It is the process of the Alchemists. It is the conversion experience whereby the cold dead human soul that dwells within the vessel of the body experiences such intense pain as a function of the false subconscious belief in the separateness of self, reaching out in pain and suffering from this pit of despair, to the light of truth of the interconnectivity of all things. The powerless disconnected life essence dwelling within the temporal physical body searches for the light of truth it knows must be there. When it reaches for the light of truth it becomes miraculously reoriented or transformed, in much the same manner as Jung describes. Reborn like lifeless water transformed into robust wine within the same vessel, or if you prefer lead to gold. The miraculous restoration of sight to see underlying truth and escape hellish deception and its impossibility of reason.

To understand the Holy Grail one may consider its function. In legend, possession of the Holy Grail is desired as one who drinks of it shall know eternal life. Well consider the following excerpt from scripture:

> *"Then Simon Peter, who had a sword, drew it and struck the high priest's servant, cutting off his right ear. (The servant's name was Malchus.) Jesus commanded Peter,*

"Put your sword away! Shall I not drink the cup the Father has given me?"

This excerpt from the Gospel according to John describes the events in the garden {Gethsemane], leading up to Christ's betrayal by Judas, his arrest and execution. The algorithm of eternal salvation in Christian doctrine is "If you accept Jesus Christ as your personal Lord and Savior you shall enjoy eternal life". From my perspective, this precept was impossible for me to accept. The physics of the proposition was seemingly irrational. As will be presented later in this work, this precept oddly enough does in fact prove a rational construct but it is rational only with the broadening of one's perspective on truth being extended past the barrier of space-time, again this concept shall be carefully built in this work so as to assist the reader in seeing and comprehending the truth and certainty of the infinite nature of life, thus transcending death. The previous excerpt from John discloses that if we, like the master seek eternal life we must, like he did, take on the mantle of suffering, or as Christ words embolden us, "Shall we not drink of the cup [of suffering] the Father has given us."

The truths which are embedded within scripture and the works of the alchemists bring us to the sight of the true eternal nature of life and of our specific life and that both are not functions of time, they are eternal. How can we comprehend the mechanisms of the observable physical world which rationalizes these truths? The central question is what are things made of? The answer is of course atoms. Well atoms in turn are constructed of smaller subatomic particles: electrons which orbit a small dense nucleus of protons and neutrons. Electrons are elemental particle which along with the other types of elemental particles are called fermions. While the more massive protons and neutrons are constructed of other types of fermions (quarks and gluons, to be specific). In my search to understand these concepts, in addition to other sources I came across a docudrama movie *"What the bleep do we know, Down the Rabbit Hole, Quantum Edition"*. Among other ideas of quantum physics, it presented an animated description of the *Double Slit Experiment*. This experiment was originally developed in the 18th Century to resolve the controversy of light: *"Is Light a Wave or a Particle"*. The findings of the refinements of this experiment in relationship to Albert Einstein's work on Special Relativity and Mass Energy Equivalence along with Niels Bohr's discoveries in the emerging field of quantum mechanics shall be discussed later in this work. Distilled, these works provide incontrovertible support for the oneness of all things and their interconnection outside the limits of space-time. On point here, it proves the oneness of all things which thereby negates the precept of death.

Lastly, prior to the economic depression of 2008 (I choose the term depression as it more accurately describes the depth of the economic disequilibrium), I was engaged in my ordinary course of business in the development of large scale multifamily residential homes throughout the state of California. The capital, approaching $1 Billion, needed to bring these projects to fruition is typically assembled sequentially through the 3 to 5 year process required to take projects of this type from inception to completion. Further it is typically assembled in concert with the largest New York based financial institutions, as was the case in my work. As 2008 approached a correction in residential real estate market conditions, through the study of leading indicators was on the horizon. As the specter of this uncertainty grew larger from 2006 through 2008 it became apparent that the correction would be sever. Twenty years prior to this time, I worked directly for a New York based bank assigned to its Dallas office. That team was charged with remediating the economic fallout upon the Bank's portfolio that the collapse of the Savings and Loan Industry precipitated throughout the Southwest. From this experience, I expected and attempted to prepare for a sizeable correction in a manner consistent with the training and experience I had in what I expected would be an equally severe downtown.

Having been thoroughly trained and schooled in all aspects of economic theory, and at the time being a devotee and ardent believer in the nobility and righteousness of laizze faire economics and the certainty with which unregulated markets would ultimately regulate themselves, I simply needed to support and recommend strategies to weather the storm, as the noble ship, the *SS Adam Smith*, fueled on the immutability of the law of supply and demand predicated upon resource scarcity, if we remained vigilant in our piloting of the floundering vessel of our business, would long course correct and return us to the promised land of Ayn Randian self-determined prosperity. The vessel sunk. Along with all of my personal financial prospects at the time. Personal bankruptcy and an indescribable hell were my lot for several years. The *SS Adam Smith* sunk, and after 240 years continues to show that capitalistic economic systems will always produce disharmony, chaos, poverty, war, injustice and crime as it is built upon a false foundation. As will be discussed later in this works economic scarcity is a function of the perception of temporal scarcity. It is a flawed and errant staring point and with certainty will always prove an unstable and disharmonious basis upon which society will perpetually know chaos, war, poverty and crime.

II. Overview

A. Why read this work? What is its Objective?

It is the author's hope that the reader heed these words throughout their journey through this work. It is expected that the seeming complexities of quantum mechanics, scriptural interpretation and foundational philosophical, governmental and economic theories may be received by some readers as overwhelming on first blush. This work has been designed principally to communicate a teaching. Stylistically, apologies are offered in advance for the repetitive nature of this presentation. However, this repetition is not by oversight it is by design. It has been designed in this manner to carefully and methodically build in a specific sequence to construct understanding of these materials.

The objective of this work is to prove to its readers the certainty of the eternal, unified and timeless nature of the universe and by extension their lives. Having so demonstrated this truth, it follows that the perspective on death than men have is fundamentally incorrect. Death, as the ending of existence shall be demonstrated here as being untrue. It is a function of paradox and deception.

By demonstrating and reinforcing the true nature of the universe, which is a unified oneness wrapped in paradox or deception the author hopes to broaden and deepen man's ability to comprehend these foundational truths so as to then be able to forge a new economic system which harmonizes with these immutable truths and in so doing vanquish disharmony, chaos, war, poverty, injustice and crime from the brotherhood of men.

B.   How will the objective be achieved?

The purpose of this study is to first demonstrate, that the nature of the universe is that of a singular cohesive field. The validity of this statement shall principally be supported through an analysis of 1.) the classical experiment in quantum physics, *The Double Slit Experiment,* 2.) Einstein's statement "Spooky Action at Distance" and it implication to special relativity and 3.) The Copenhagen Interpretation of Quantum Superposition. In addition to an analysis of scientific theory, the cohesiveness of the universe will be supported through an analysis of scripture. Once the singular nature of the universe has been thus demonstrated, it reveals the essence of a universal existential impossibility. Stated alternatively "One Thing Cannot Exist." The essence of existence is that of a series of interactions, or experiences over the variable of time. In logic, the singular nature of the universe is such that existence, or stated alternatively, the interaction of more than one element, is impossible outside of paradox, as there is but one element: the universal field. The nature of existence, or stated alternatively, subject/observer interaction, is a paradoxical function, which shall herein be demonstrated mathematically and through a series of visual constructs

Having demonstrated the essential nature of the singular field and the paradoxical nature of existence, or stated alternatively consciousness, an evaluation of the nature of human consciousness shall be constructed upon this logic. In particular, the birth of human reasoning, its implications as a function of paradox, or stated alternatively, deception. Based upon this foundationally paradoxical construct, a survey of human history focused on social and economic systems will be evaluated. This survey shall be evidence supporting the premise that all previously instituted systems have proved unjust and unsustainable as a direct function of the theories underlying these systems being foundationally disharmonious to the true interconnected, unified and paradoxical nature of the universe.

The objective of this writing is to present evidence of an overwhelming nature that demonstrates that the native state of the universe is "One-ness" wrapped in deception. It is by its construct paradoxical. It is the duty of this generation to rationalize this paradox and in so doing recognize that the socio-economic construct of the early 21st century is an affront to natural law as this system has root assumptions, namely scarcity and rationality of economic markets that are both false. They therefor have and can do nothing other than result in a society in which war and poverty will remain a constant. We shall overcome this affront to Natural Law and the brotherhood of all men, so enlightened, shall empower one another, as Jefferson suggested, to throw off our old despotic system and install new guards for our future security.

III. Singularity

A. Introduction

The purpose this text's section on the Singularity is to help the reader construct the ability to see the true nature of the universe's "One-ness". A convergence of man's ability to comprehend quantum realities and mechanics alongside scripture points us in the direction of the oneness of all things. To begin laying the foundation of this truth so that it may be seen and understood broadly at depth, consider the following: To explore the notion of "God (the "Singularity")", one may determine to identify, in a clearly comprehensible manner, the following two questions: 1.) Does God exist? and 2.) "What are the essential and distinguishable characteristics of God? Consider the following observation:

> *"God is either everything or else he is nothing. God either is or he isn't... (Alcoholics Anonymous (2001), p.53"*

The preceding proposition regarding the nature of God presents a useful framework to explore God's essence and existence in flawless logic. Room for only two possibilities on this foundational question exists: "God either is or he isn't". The sum

28

of the probability of these two outcomes on the question of God's existence precisely equals 100%. Further, truth will ultimately be observed such that one alternative is 100% true and the other is 100% false. It seems a small extension of these unequivocal observations to then assert that if "God Is" he is everything, and if "God Is Not", he is nothing. The purpose of this text will be dedicated to demonstrating that through logic and a preponderance of supporting evidence, that the alternative *"God is and is therefore everything"* is true. As a function of this truth, the author intends to deconstruct the *Foundational Existential Paradox* which arises out of the truth of a universe underlain by the essence of an all-powerful, omnipotent God.

Einstein, in 1905 demonstrated in: *"Does the inertia of a body depend upon its energy-content?"* one of his *Annus Mirabilis* ("Miraculous Year") Papers, mass-energy equivalence, or stated alternatively the interchangeability between mass and energy. It follows therefore that God, being all powerful is in fact all things (All Powerful = All Matter; and/or Omnipotent = Omnipresent), pursuant to Einstein's demonstration of mass-energy equivalence. Stated alternatively. *"God is Everything"* and is the Oneness of all things, the Singularity and the cohesive universal field, this follows as indisputable logic.

The following is an excerpt of a letter written by Einstein in 1950, to comfort a bereaving parent upon the loss of a child

> *"A human being is a part of the whole called by us universe, a part limited in time and space. He experiences himself, his thoughts and feeling as something separated from the rest, a kind of optical delusion of his consciousness. This delusion is a kind of prison for us, restricting us to our personal desires and to affection for a few persons nearest to us. Our task must be to free ourselves from this prison by widening our circle of compassion to embrace all living creatures and the whole of nature in its beauty."* (Einstein, A., Calaprice, A., (2005))

A final thought to conclude this introduction of the Singularity is the spiritual concept of ATONEMENT (Hyperdictionary.com (2015)), or broken down...AT-ONE-MENT. In a religious sense, atonement means "*at-one-ment*", the state of being "*at one*", or being reconciled with the universe as Singularity, or stated alternatively God. We as human beings by design, fall from an atoned state of consciousness. In the section of this text on the *Gestational State of Human Conscious* we shall further explore this phenomenon. The purpose of introducing the concept of atonement here is to reinforce the observations coming from both scientific and spiritual study that all is indeed one. The society of man has lived and continues to live within the bounds of socioeconomic constructs which are a function of the *Universal Paradox* (this concept will likewise be dimensioned in a separate section of this text). It follows therefore that these constructs must be at odds with and inconsistent with the foundational truth of the Singularity or Oneness. As such we have constructed and continue to maintain socio-economic systems in which the prospects for harmony and peace are irrational expectation and that to choose to continue the current set of socioeconomic norms would serve only to continue the reality of war and poverty which is the inescapable result of all socioeconomic systems that are not atoned. The principal root assumption of capitalistic economics is scarcity. Economic resources are assumed to exist in a fundamentally scarce quantity. It is this scarcity that theoretically leads to price equilibrium as a function of supply and demand and it is through this process that man theoretically will arrive at a marketplace for these commodities that is inherently rational. The truth of the

Singularity or the Omnipresence of God or the Oneness of the Universe negates the validity of the scarcity assumption which is the foundational assumption of all capitalistic economic systems. All elements, in their oneness exist in a perfect state of harmony, distinguishable from a state of scarcity. It follows therefore that scarcity of resources is unequivocally untrue and that all equilibriums which arise from this false precept are inherently unstable. The continuation of war, poverty and crime within the brotherhood of man serves as compelling evidence in support of these logically derived truths.

B. Double Slit Experiment

The purpose of this section of the text is to provide a brief overview of the history of the classic "Double Slit Experiment" and its usefulness in seeing universal connectivity or the Singularity.

The original double slit experiment was designed in the early 19th century by the English Physician, Philosopher and Scientist, Thomas Young (1773 – 1829). Young's intent was to uncover the true nature of light, *was it a wave or a particle*? In the 17th century, Sir Isaac Newton (1642 – 1727) had demonstrated that light behaved as a particle, which he called a corpuscle. At the same time one of his contemporaries, Christian Huygens (1629 – 1695) had demonstrated that light behaved as a wave. The answer to the question "Is light a wave or a particle" remained in dispute.

Young, studied Newton's *Opticks (1790).* In this work, Newtown experimentally demonstrated light's behavior to be that of a particle (or a corpuscle as he referred to it therein). Young noted that there were a series of circumstances where Newtown's conclusion broke down. In particular, light's behavior regarding reflections and refractions of different colors did not conform to Newton's findings.

Young designed his experiment whereby a light source would project through double slits. If light were a particle, it would project along a screen as two bright bands (lining up behind the slit openings). However, if light were a wave, the two slits would each produce a separate wave. Troughs of one wave would cancel with peaks of other waves and so on. If light were a wave, the two waves would result in an interference pattern upon the screen, which is precisely what it did. Game over, LIGHT IS A WAVE.

Not so fast, Einstein refuted the wave theory of light. Consider the following excerpt from Rigden (2005):

In the March paper of 1905, Einstein directly challenged the orthodoxy of physics: orthodoxy that had grown and strengthened for over a century; orthodoxy that rested on bedrock experiment and far-ranging theory. All physicists in 1905 knew what light was. Whether from the Sun or an incandescent light bulb, light was known to be a wave; that is, a succession of equally spaced crests separated by equally spaced troughs where the distance between the crests (or the troughs) determined the light's color. All scientists knew, without doubt, that light originated at a source, spread out evenly and continuously through all the space accessible to it, and propagated from place to place as electromagnetic crests and troughs. Light was called an electromagnetic wave or, more generally, electromagnetic radiation. In 1905, the wave nature of light was an established, incontrovertible fact. In the face of this universally held knowledge, Einstein proposed that light was not a continuous wave, but consisted of localized particles. As Einstein wrote in the introduction to his March paper, "According to the assumption to be contemplated here, when a light ray is spreading from a point, the energy is not distributed continuously over ever-increasing spaces, but consists of a finite number of energy quanta that are localized in points in space, move without dividing, and can be absorbed or generated only as a whole." This sentence has been called "the most

Essentially, light contains energy (quanta) which "can be absorbed or generated ONLY as a whole", turning over yet again our understanding of the nature of light. Einstein's observation regarding the properties of light respecting energy stand, while at the same time they do not refute the wave characteristics of light. Einstein's observation on light, principally with respect to the photoelectric effect, which basically provides that the energy within photons can be sufficient to displace electrons of metallic objects, those electrons are then referred to as photoelectrons.

Einstein's findings stimulated a series of refinements to the Double Slit experiment. It was thought that if an experiment could be designed in which a single photon of light could be shot through the slit filter it could not interfere with itself and would behave as a particle and result in two bright bands and not an interference spectrum. That has since been accomplished in the laboratory, but single photon double slit experiments result in the same interference pattern. What is the single photon interfering with scientists wondered. They then decided to place detectors at each of the slit openings. **THIS IS WHERE THE FUNDAMENTAL NATURE OF THE UNIVERSE REVEALS ITSELF. WHEN DETECTORS WERE PLACED ON THE SLITS THE PROJECTED PATTERN CHANGED TO TWO BRIGHT BANDS AND NO LONGER PROJECTED AS AN INTERFERENCE PATTERN.**

LIGHT IS AWARE OF OBSERVATION. WHEN IT IS NOT BEING OBSERVED, IT IS A WAVE IN QUANTUM SUPERPOSITION (TO BE EXPLAINED IN A LATER SECTION OF THIS TEXT); BUT WHEN IT IS OBSERVED THE WAVE FUNCTION COLLAPSES AND MANIFESTS AS A PHOTON.

<u>**SUMMARY**</u> – There exists a cause and effect relationship between light and consciousness or conscious observation. When light is not consciously observed it is a wave in quantum superposition, the act of observing light causes the collapse of the wave function resulting in that light alternating its mode from wave to photon as a direct function of conscious observation.

The purpose of the forgoing is to construct for the reader the ability to see that the universe is, at the quantum or elemental scale one interconnected, entangled field. The operations of consciousness upon light are an illustration of that quantum entanglement.

C.   Quantum Superposition: *The Copenhagen Interpretation*

Young's 18th Century design of the Double Slit Experiment provided seemingly conclusive evidence that light is a wave, and only a wave. Certain 20th century discoveries, such as observations on the Photoelectric effect suggested that the "wave-only" theory of light was incomplete. Einstein observed that as light exerts force on certain metals sufficient to eject photoelectrons from those metals it must have mass to exert that force and must therefore be a particle (photon). The modified double slit experiments referred to in the previous section demonstrated that light behaves as a wave and a particle, but not both at the same time. Further it is the very act of conscious observation that causes the collapse of the wave such that it then manifests as a particle (photon), with distinguishable and measurable mass.

During the 1920s, Bohr's contributions to the development of quantum mechanical theory were conducted in his institute located in Copenhagen, hence the name. At that time Werner Heisenberg was an assistant at Bohr's institute. In this capacity he (Heisenberg) delivered a series of lectures on the new field of Quantum Mechanics. These lectures became the basis of *The*

Physical Principles of the Quantum Theory, Heisenberg's 1930 publication on the subject.

The name *The Copenhagen Interpretation* falsely and inadvertently suggests a series of other interpretations of Quantum Mechanics. To the contrary, prior to his 1955 publication of *Physics and Philosophy* (Freire, 2005) Heisenberg stated:

> *"I avow that the term 'Copenhagen Interpretation' is not happy since it could suggest that there are other interpretations, like Bohm assumes. We agree, of course, that the other interpretations are nonsense, and I believe that this is clear in my book, and in previous papers..."*
> (Freire, 2005)

The Copenhagen Interpretation is discussed here as it provides an excellent basis to help visualize and reinforce the interconnected and interactive nature of consciousness. In particular, the term Quantum Superposition was used in the previous section. Quantum Superposition is an element of *The Copenhagen Interpretation* of Quantum Mechanics. To draw from the previously discussed 20th century modified Double Slit Experiment, which introduced detectors at the slits, Quantum

Superposition is the term used to describe the infinite number of probabilistic states a photon can exist in wave form prior to observation. The modified Double Slit Experiment demonstrated that light was a wave as evidenced by the projected interference pattern prior to observation. However, when the slit was directly observed, the light wave collapsed and reduced to its distinguishable particle (photon) state as evidenced by the two bright bands aligned with the slit openings. This supports the assertion that it was the observation itself which caused the collapse or reduction of the wave in Quantum Superposition into a distinguishable photon. *The Copenhagen Interpretation* holds that it is the conscious observation itself that causes a light wave in quantum superposition to collapse and reduce into a photon with distinguishable mass. **IT THEN FOLLOWS THAT CONSCIOUS OBSERVATION CAUSES THE MANIFESTATION OF LIGHT AND MATTER.**

D. Quantum Entanglement: *Einstein's "Spooky Action at Distance"*

As was demonstrated in the previous section on Quantum Superposition, it is the very act of

conscious observation which collapses a light wave from its state of Quantum Superposition into a particle or photon having a distinguishable mass. The *"Spookiness"* expands! From the late 1920s, Einstein and Bohr entered into a schism that would last the rest of their lives over the seeming contradictions between Quantum Mechanics and Special Relativity. The schism arose as follows: a central element in Quantum Mechanics is a phenomenon referred to as Quantum

Entanglement. It has been consistently demonstrated that pairs of particles may be entangled with one another. This entanglement seems to arise as a function of the original conscious observation of a wave in quantum superposition, which causes an initial collapsing and reduction of the wave in quantum superposition into a series of photons. When such observations occur in close proximity in space-time they cause such entanglements. Particles so entangled with one another, which at some future time are located at great distances, continue to cause instantaneous changes

42

to their twin particle. This phenomenon is always validated when tested, it is not disputed.

As this bridge was first encountered in the late 1920s, approximately 20 years after Einstein's work on Special Relativity, Einstein received this discovery with great skepticism. He recognized that particles at distance that are entangled in this manner, can interact at speeds faster than light. Einstein concluded that this must either be incorrect or incomplete. In the mid 1930s, Einstein, Boris Podolsky and Nathan Rosen set out to refute the validity of quantum mechanics or alternatively expand or complete it. This study is referred to as the EPR Paradox (named for the Scientists). The conclusion they reached validated that the understanding of quantum mechanics at the time was fundamentally incomplete and that since nothing can travel through space-time faster than the speed of light, they concluded that the interaction must therefore occur as a result of a "hidden variable" outside of space-time, or non-locally, or as Einstein describes it "Spooky Action at Distance".

In the 1960s, while at CERN laboratory, John Bell validated that quantum mechanics are an intrinsically "non-local" phenomenon, meaning the nature of the entanglements are an element of reality outside the limitations of the four dimensions of space-time. All mechanics within the four dimensions of space and time must obey the laws described in Einstein's Special Relativity. However, the operations of waves in quantum superposition, consciousness, conscious observation, Wave function collapse, reduction to particles and the resulting phenomenon of quantum entanglement (or if you prefer *"spooky connection at distance"), are inherently nonlocal* or stated alternatively transcend space-time.

TO SUMMARIZE, THE OPERATIONS OF QUANTUM MECHANICS DEMONSTRATE THE ESSENTIAL AND TRUE NATURE OF THE SINGULARITY OR UNIVERSAL FIELD AS IT EXISTS OUTSIDE THE BOUNDS OF SPACE-TIME. IT FURTHER DEMONSTRATES THAT THE SINGULARITY PENETRATES SPACETIME FROM A NON-LOCAL ORIGIN AS A FUNCTION OF ITS INTERACTION WITH CONSCIOUSNESS OR CONSCIOUS OBSERVATION. STATED

ALTERNATIVELY, TWO PHOTONS LOCATED A GREAT DISTANCES FROM ONE ANOTHER DEMONSTRATE A HIDDEN CONNECTION THAT CAN TRANSMIT FORCES APPLIED TO ONE OF THE ENTANGLED PARTICLES, INSTANTLY RESULTING IN AN EFFECT ON THE REMOTE PARTICLE AT SPEEDS WHICH EXCEED THE SPEED OF LIGHT.

E.   Scripture: Genesis 1: 3

"And God said, "Let there be light," and there was light.

Genesis 1: 3

The purpose of this section of the text is to increase the readers' ability to see the reality and truth of the Singularity. To review from previous sections, what we know beyond doubt is:

1.) Light exists as a wave in quantum superposition outside of space-time prior to observation.

2.) The act of observing the light wave in quantum superposition is what causes the wave function to collapse and the light to manifest in space-time as a photon.

3.) Following the collapse of the wave function and the manifestation of light as a photon within the bounds of space time, other photons collapsing in relative proximity within space-time exist remain connected in a state of quantum entanglement. Meaning that at some arbitrary future time quantumly entangled particles, regardless of vast distances between them within the four-dimensions of space-time, cause changes in their twin particle's behavior at speeds which exceeding the speed of light.

It follows therefore, as Bell stated in his 1960 work on quantum entanglement that quantum mechanics is intrinsically non-local (meaning these mechanics occur beyond the boundary of space-time).

In this text, an Omnipresence and Omnipotent Creative Consciousness has been used synonymously with the word God as well as the word Singularity.

VERSE 3 OF GENESIS 1 PRECISELY MIRRORS QUANTUM MECHANICS. IN THAT IN GENESIS IT IS THE ACT OF GOD OBERVING LIGHT, THAT CAUSES THE LIGHT TO BE. TRULY THE SPOOKIEST OF CONNECTIONS, AS THE DISCOVERY OF QUANTUM MECHANICS POST DATES THE WRITING OF GENESIS BY THOUSANDS OF YEARS. THE ANSWER TO THE QUESTION OF HOW THE AUTHOR OF GENESIS KNEW ABOUT THE PRINCIPLES OF QUANTUM MECHANICS THOUSANDS OF YEARS BEFORE ITS DISCOVERY IS WELL BEYOND THE SCOPE OF THIS TEXT,

NEVERTHELESS, AS SCRIPTURE HAS SERVED MAN FOR MILLENIA AS A SOURCE FROM WHICH MAN CAN DISCOVER TRUTH, THE CONGRUENCY BETWEEN THE PRICIPLES OF QUANTUM MECHANICS AND THIS VERSE OF GENESIS ARE UNDENIABLE.

F. Conclusion

The purpose of the section on the Singularity is to assist the reader in visualizing the essence of the universal field of consciousness or the Singularity. Consider the following

1. The Introduction to this section offered a process in logic to support the notion of the "oneness" or interconnectivity of the universe. With respect to the question of the existence of God, there are but two possibilities: 1.) "God Is" or 2.) "God Is Not". It seems foundational that if "God Is" the singular essential characteristic of God is Omnipotence, it is seemingly definitional that if God is not all-powerful then it cannot be God. Proceeding from this starting place, if we accept the alternative that "God Is" and by definition Omnipotent, and since per Einstein, mass and energy are interchangeable, God must also be all things, or Omnipresent.

2. The preceding logic is exacting but it is predicated upon the assumption that the "God Is" alternative is true. If we substitute God for the terms universal field,

or Singularity or as was coined in the EPR Paradox the "non-local hidden variable" we discover irrefutable evidence supporting the interconnectivity, or stated alternatively the "oneness" of all things. This cohesiveness, described in the EPR Paradox as the non-local hidden variable, is referred to as non-local not because it is not close-by or local in the everyday sense of the word local, but because the hidden variable (or force) cannot have a location within the four-dimensions of space-time. This is true as the hidden variable is a medium through which forces can be asserted between quantumly entangled particles at speeds exceeding the speed of light which, per Special Relativity cannot occur within the bounds of Space-time.

3. It has thus been demonstrated that outside space-time elemental particles are entangled with one another. All objects and all matter, and all galaxies and all people are constructed of these entangled elemental particles. It follows therefore that all objects and all matter and

all galaxies and all people are entangled or interconnected, or stated alternatively, are manifestations of a singular wave in quantum superposition (outside space-time), which at some time in the past were individually observed causing collapses of the wave function creating individual particles. Those particle now operating in space-time remain rooted, entangled and interconnected to the force existing beyond space-time.

BASED UPON THE FOREGOING, EVIDENCE EXISTS AND HAS BEEN EXPIRIMNTALLY DEMONSTRATED THAT THE OPERATIONS OF QUANTUM MECHANICS LAY OUTSIDE SPACE-TIME. OUTSIDE OF SPACE-TIME, ENERGY AND MASS MANIFEST INTO SPACE-TIME AS A RESULT OF HAVING BEEN OBSERVED FROM WITHIN SPACE-TIME. AFTER MATTER OR ENERGY MANIFESTS INSIDE SPACE-TIME IN THIS MANNER, IT REMAINS ENTANGELD OUTSIDE SPACETIME. STATED ALTERNATIVELY, ALL MATTER AND ENERGY IN THE UNIVERSE REMAINS QUANTUMLY ENTANGLED OUTSIDE SPACETIME,

AND THROUGH THIS ENTANGLEMENT ALL THINGS ARE INTERCONNECTED, OR STATED ALTERNATIVELY, ALL THINGS ARE ONE.

REFERENCES

Alcoholics Anonymous. (2001). Alcoholics Anonymous, 4th Edition. New York: A.A. World Services.

Einstein, A., Calaprice, A., & Einstein, A. (2005). *The new quotable Einstein*. Princeton, N.J: Princeton University Press.

"Atonement," Retrieved on December 12, 2015 from HyperDictionary.com, at: http://www.hyperdictionary.com/

Rigden, J. (2005). *Einstein 1905: The standard of greatness*. Cambridge, Mass.: Harvard University Press.

Freire, O., Jr., (2005) "Science and exile: David Bohm, the hot times of the Cold War, and his struggle for a new interpretation of quantum mechanics", *Historical Studies on the Physical and Biological Sciences*, Volume 36, Number 1, 2005, pp. 31–35.

IV. Existential Paradox

In the previous section on Singularity we demonstrated that, as was referred to in the EPR Paradox, the workings of quantum mechanics are dependent upon "hidden variables" which exist in wave form in quantum superposition outside of space-time, or "non-locally". The nature of "the hidden variables" as well as the behavior of elemental particles collapsing into space-time as a direct result of being observed, is that the particles remain connected despite distances, even vast distances between them. Everything is constructed of these elemental particles, it follows therefore that everything is interconnected and through interconnection everything is one. This notion is not new, consider the following observations:

"Quantum physics thus reveals a basic oneness of the universe."

Erwin Schrodinger

(source unknown)

"A human being is a part of the whole called by us universe, a part limited in time and space. He experiences himself, his thoughts and feeling as something separated from the rest, a kind of optical delusion of his consciousness. This delusion is a kind of prison for us, restricting us to our personal desires and to affection for a few

persons nearest to us. Our task must be to free ourselves from this prison by widening our circle of compassion to embrace all living creatures and the whole of nature in its beauty."
Einstein (A. Calaprice (2005) "The New Quotable Einstein")

"Quantum theory thus...shows that we cannot decompose the world into independently existing smallest units. As we penetrate into matter, nature does not show us any isolated "building blocks," but rather appears as a complicated web of relations between the various parts of the whole."

Fritjof Capra (The Tao of Physics)

"....it is a strange thing that most of the feeling we call religious, most of the mystical out crying which is one of the most prized and used and desired reactions of our species, is really the understanding and the attempt to say that man is related to the whole thing, related inextricably to all reality, known and unknowable. This is a simple thing to say, but the profound feeling of it made a Jesus, a St. Augustine, a St. Francis, a Roger Bacon, a Charles Darwin, and an Einstein. Each of them in his own tempo and with his own voice discovered and reaffirmed with

astonishment the knowledge that all things are one thing and that one thing is all things—plankton, a shimmering phosphorescence on the sea and the spinning planets and an expanding universe, all bound together by the elastic string of time."

John Steinbeck (The Log from the Sea of Cortez)

"One of the most prospective directions of study of C.G. Jung's synchronicity phenomenon is reviewed considering the latest achievements of modern science. The attention is focused mainly on quantum entanglement and related phenomenon quantum coherence and quantum superposition. It is shown that the quantum non-locality capable of solving the Einstein-Podolsky-Rosen paradox represents one of the most adequate physical mechanisms in terms of conformity with Jung's synchronicity hypothesis."

Igor V. Limar

(Carl G. Jung's Synchronicity And Quantum Entanglement: Schrödinger's Cat 'Wanders' Between Chromosomes)

The body of work on the nature of "existence" is voluminous and often contradictory. However, what seems inescapable is a description of existence as a series of experiences over time. Observations on "oneness" seem to negate the possibility of existence, albeit falsely so. For if existence is indeed a series of experiences what does the "universal one" have experiences with? It leaves us with the following paradox:

1.) All is one;

2.) Existence as a series of experiences or interactions requires more than one element;

3.) There is not more than one element;

4.) The foregoing are mutually exclusive, yet both are true;

5.) It follows therefore that the existence of the universe balances on Paradox

V. Rationalizing the Universal Paradox

A. Introduction

In the previous sections we demonstrated that the field of Quantum Mechanics has opened a portal through which man can perceive and comprehend the oneness of all things based upon experimental evidence and deduction. The oneness of all things has been apparent and cleverly hidden from man throughout the ages in the most diabolical of hiding places: under our nose. Furthermore, oneness lays close to the root of many of the world's ancient belief systems as it was known to enlightened masters through the ages. Consider the following excerpts:

> *"Hear, O Israel: The Lord our God, the Lord is ONE."*
>
> *Deuteronomy 6:4*

> *"He is the one God, hidden in all beings, all-pervading, the Self within all beings, watching over all works, dwelling in all beings, the witness, the perceiver, the only one, free from qualities."*
>
> *Quran 112*

"He is the Sole Supreme Being; of eternal manifestation; Creator, Immanent Reality; Without Fear, Without Rancor; Timeless Form; Unincarnated; Self-existent; Realized by the grace of the Holy Preceptor.`"

Svetasvatara Upanishad 6.11

"When I saw him, I fell at his feet as if I were dead. But he laid his right hand on me and said, "Don't be afraid! I am the First and the Last. I am the living ONE. I died, but look—I am alive forever and ever! And I hold the keys of death and the grave"

Revelations 1:17-18

"In the beginning the Word already existed. The Word was with God, and the Word was God. He existed in the beginning with God. God created everything through him, and nothing was created except through him. The Word gave life to everything that was created, and his life brought light to everyone. The light shines in the darkness, and the darkness can never extinguish it"

John 1:1-4

"Absolute truth is indestructible. Being indestructible, it is eternal. Being eternal, it is self-existent. Being self-existent, it is infinite. Being infinite, it is vast and deep. Being vast and deep, it is transcendental and intelligent. It is because it is vast and deep that it contains all existence. It is because it is transcendental and intelligent that it embraces all existence. It is because it is infinite and eternal that it fulfills or perfects all existence. In vastness and depth it is like the Earth. In transcendental intelligence it is like Heaven. Infinite and eternal, it is the Infinite itself. Such being the nature of absolute truth, it manifests itself without being seen; it produces effects without motion; it accomplishes its ends without action."

Tao Te Ching, 23

Arrived at the recognition of the truthfulness of universal cohesion or oneness, it was then demonstrated that from this foundation, the nature of existence is inherently Paradoxical as:

1) All is one;

2) Existence as a series of experiences or interactions requires more than one element;

3) There is not more than one element

4) The foregoing are mutually exclusive, yet both are true

5) It follows therefore that the existence of the universe balances on Paradox

The purpose of this section of the text will present several visual examples which are designed to help the reader visualize and distinguish different means through which man observes and gains understanding and more importantly the limits in which that understanding remains valid. These different methods of observation are:

1.) Based upon his senses alone without deductive reasoning "Unreasoned Observation";

2.) Based upon his senses and deductive reasoning "Ordinary Observation" and

3.) Based upon his deductive reasoning alone "Non-Ordinary Observation'.

"Unreasoned Observation" or sensory knowledge discloses limited yet valuable understanding. For example, I need not deductively reason through the process through which my skin will become damaged and charred by a hot stove. Pondering the relative merits of ointments, their proper application healing time

and other such contemplations are unnecessary in extracting the only information which is required for an immediate response. All I need understand is intense heat causes pain. Instantaneous removal of hand is the maximally enlightened response. **IT IS IMPORTANT TO NOTE THAT THIS MEANS OF OBSERVATION IS SHARED AMONG MEN AND BEASTS.**

"Ordinary Observation" results in broader understanding of a subject than does "Unreasoned Observation", yet still has limits. It is through this form of observation than man learned how the farm, build city's, conceive the idea of money as a means to safeguard and support economic efficiencies and justice and construct rockets capable of escaping the earth's gravity to then look upon it in its totality for the first time. **IT IS IMPORTANT TO NOTE THAT THIS MEANS OF OBSERVTION, BASED UPON CONSIDERATION OF ALL APPARENT DATA, IS UNIQUE WITHIN THE SPECIES OF MAN UPON THE EARTH. OTHER BEASTS OF THE EARTH DO NOT DEMONSTRATE BEHAVIORS WHICH SUGGEST THEY HAVE THE CAPACITY OF DEDUCTIVE REASONING.**

"Non-Ordinary Observation", results in full and complete understanding. It is limitless as it is simple. The millennia long process of "Ordinary Observation" has been a journey over which man has grown and expanded his deductive reasoning capacity through increasing complexity. Over this path man has arrived at a destination. That destination is the emergence and widening of "Non-Ordinary Observation" capability. This method of observation exists for man to be able to see through and understand the "Oneness" of all things. This can only be understood by having a practical ability to see past the barrier between space-time and the fifth dimension. Enlightened masters throughout the ages had seemingly been able to access this sight intuitively. In the 20th and 21st century we can see these transcendental truths through analyses of data gathered in studies of quantum mechanics. Through deduction we prove the truth of this extra-dimensional interconnectivity. **AS WILL BE DETAILED IN THE SECTION OF THIS TEXT ON THE GESTATIONAL PERIOD OF HUMAN REASONING, WE WILL DEMONSTRATE THAT THROUGH THE EXPANSION OF THIS SIGHT, CAPACITY AND UNDERSTANDING WITHIN THE BROTHERHOOD OF**

MAN, WE WILL USHER IN AN ERA IN WHICH WE WILL BE ABLE TO UNDERSTAND THAT DEATH IS AN ILLUSION. IT FOLLOWS THEN, IF TIME IS NOT SCARCE THE MEANS THROUGH WHICH HARMONIOUSLY ABUNDENT RESOURCES ARE CULTIVATED AND SHARED TO SUPPORT LIFE MUST CHANGE SO THESE MEANS ARE NO LONGER BASED UPON THE PESTILENTIAL AND FALSE PREMISES OF DEATH AND SCARCITY BUT RATHER THEY SHLL BE BASED UPON THE TRUTH OF ABUNDANCE AND INTERCONNECTIVITY.

Lastly, if the universe is indeed "One" as has been demonstrated here, this truth must be mathematically demonstrable. This section will conclude with a mathematical proof which not only demonstrates the oneness of the universe but also rationalizes the existential paradox.

> *"A new type of thinking is essential if mankind is to survive and move toward higher levels"*
>
> *("Atomic Education Urged by Einstein", New York Times 1946)*

B. Examples of different types of human observation

In the introduction to this section we created distinctions between the different means through which man observes subjects so that he may gain understanding. The three methods were described as follows:

1.) Based upon his senses alone without deductive reasoning "Unreasoned Observation";

2.) Based upon his senses and deductive reasoning "Ordinary Observation" and

3.) Based upon his deductive Reasoning alone "Non-Ordinary Observation'.

The purpose of this section is to assist the reader in seeing how the different methods of observation disclose varying levels of understanding. When we extrapolate from a starting point of a limited understanding on a subject that we obtained either through Unreasoned or Ordinary Observation, we can often develop misunderstanding and false conclusions. To reinforce the idea that observation can result in misleading and incomplete understanding, consider the following:

i.   Atoms / "Empty-Solid" Objects – Essentially, all matter that we observe is constructed of atoms, which in turn interact to become molecules, which in turn interact to become: rocks, trees, fish, people, planets, stars and galaxies. Stated alternatively: Everything I see is made of Atoms.

Atoms are constructed of electrons, protons and neutrons (which themselves are constructed of more elemental particles, but for our purpose here, that topic is outside the scope of the discussion). The volume of an atom is comprised of a very dense core or nucleus made of protons and neutrons. This nucleus is surrounded by a series of "electron shells". Within the electron shells, electrons orbit the nucleus. The electrons themselves have relatively tiny mass (about 1/2000 that of a proton or neutron), so the volume of the electron shells are almost entirely empty.

The volume of the electron shells account for 99.9999999999999% of the total volume of the atom; and as the electron shells are essential empty space, it follows that the volume of all atoms is 99.9999999999999% empty space. To reinforce this visual, the percent of empty space within an atom is roughly equivalent to the percent of the solar system that is empty space.

WHY IS THIS USEFUL? IT PROVIDES CLEAR PROOF THAT WHAT I SEE, "SOLID OBJECTS" ARE AT THEIR ESSENCE 99.9999999999999% EMPTY SPACE, IT FOLLOWS THEREFORE THAT WHAT I OBSERVE WITH MY SENSES AND UNDERLYING TRUTH ARE NOT THE SAME THING.

ii. Round (Spherical) v. Flat Earth:

The earth is spherical. The only way of observing this through senses only is to launch a rocket into space and see it. From my vantage point on the surface of the earth, the limits of my vision is approximately 3 miles and within that limitations it is not possible for the unaided eye to observe the curvature of the spherical earth. So based upon my physical senses alone I must conclude that the earth is flat, which is fundamentally untrue.

The notion of the earth being spherical or round is ancient. Evidence of the theory of a spherical or round earth goes back at least as far as Pythagoras (6th Century BCE). Seems as if the observed patterns of the movement of the stars throughout the seasons of the year, as well as observations made by travelers on long journeys, caused early man to gain the notion that regardless of what he saw with his eyes (a "Flat Earth") there was subtle evidence which contradicted his senses and that through experimentation and deduction his reason empowered him to transcend the limitations of his senses to see through to fundamental truth. **AGAIN THIS ILLUSTRATES THAT IF I CAN ONLY RELY UPON MY SENSES TO**

UNDERSTAND A SUBJECT, MY UNDERSTANDING OF THAT SUBJECT WILL BE HIGHLY LIMITED. FOR EXAMPLE, A SMALL PORTION OF THE EARTH, IS INDEED, PRACTICLLY SPEAKING FLAT, THAT PORTION IS PROXIMATE IN SIZE TO THE EXTENT OF MY PHYSICAL SIGHT. WITHIN THAT TIGHT LIMITED CONTEXT, WHAT I OBSERVE WITH MY SENSES IS NOT QUITE FALSE, IT IS MERELY INCOMPLETE. IT IS ONLY WHEN I ATTEMPT TO TAKE THIS LIMITED SCOPE OF UNDERSTANDING, AND EXPAND IT TO A UNIVERSAL TRUTH THAT IT BECOMES MISLEADING, INACCURATE AND FALSE.

The two preceding examples are quite simple. The broader truths discovered in each of those examples, are a function of observation as well as deductive reasoning. In each instance, the subject is a physical element within the bounds of space-time.

Through the scientific method, I can through sensory input and deductive reason come to understand the true essence of subjects that reside in space-time. What happens when we attempt to gain understanding of a subject that resides outside of space-time, all we can observe is what occurs in space-time? At the barrier between the four-dimensions of space time and the upper transcendent dimension, or as it was described in the EPR Paradox the "non-local hidden variable" we then lose all use of the input of our senses, we must rely only upon deductive reasoning. Stated alternatively, it seems that the eyes cannot penetrate the barrier between space-time and the transcendent dimension but the mind can. Consider this final example:

    iii.   Table Demonstration – The purpose of this example is to provide a visual image of how the "non-local hidden variable" as evidenced by the behaviors we have previously described as quantum entanglement, or "Spooky Connection at Distance" can be observed as a function of "non-ordinary" observation.

Visualize if you will a table. Fixed to the edge of the table on all sides is a dark curtain. You cannot see what is beneath the curtain. You can only see the top of the table. You notice four holes in the top of the table. After a moment you then observe different colored cloth projecting through each of the holes. Through the Northeast quadrant hole you observe a red cloth, through the Southeast quadrant whole you observe a white cloth, through the Southwest quadrant whole you observe a blue cloth and through the Northwest quadrant hole you observe a green cloth.

This is the only information you may have about this system. The question is how many cloths are there? From your perspective, the correct and obvious answer is 4, red, white, blue and green cloths.

However, the system was designed to make it impossible to make observations beyond a constructed barrier, the table top. Prior to the experiment a single large cloth was dyed four different colors in sections and an assistant sat under the cloth and table to push the different colored sections of the cloth through the holes in the table sections. Clearly there is only one interconnected cloth but the connection exists beyond a barrier through which observation is not permitted.

AS YOU CAN SEE, THE ENTIRETY OF THE CLOTH FROM THIS EXAMPLE REPRESENTS THE WAVE FUNCTION IN QUANTUM SUPERPOSITION BEYOND THE SPACE-TIME BARRIER. WE WERE NOT ALLOWED TO OBSERVE THE COHESIVENESS OF THE CLOTH, AND WE CANNOT OBSERVE THE WAVE FUNCTION IN QUANTUM SUPERPOSITION. LIKEWISE, THE DIFFERENT COLORED SECTIONS OF CLOTH APPEAR AS SEPARATE CLOTHS

JUST AS ELEMENTARY PARTICALS WHICH MANIFEST IN SPACE-TIME AS A FUNCTION OF OBSERVATIONAPPEAR AS DISTINCT AND SEPARATE. IN BOTH INSTANCES THE SEEMINGLY DISCONNECTED ELEMENTS, EITHER THE CLOTHS OR THE PARTICLES, REMAIN INTERCONNECTED ON THE OTHER SIDE OF A BARRIER THROUGH WHICH OBSERVATION IS NOT PERMITTED.

BY EXPERIMENTATION AND DEDUCTIVE REASONING WE HAVE DISCOVERED THE REALITY OF QUANTUM ENTANGLEMENT. WE NOW KNOW THAT ELEMENTAL PARTICLES REMAIN CONNECTED DESPITE OUR INABILITY TO OBSERVE THEIR CONNECTION. THIS UNDERSTANDING OF TRUTH HAS BEEN ACHEIEVED THROUGH WHAT I

PREVIOUSLY DESCRIBED AS "NON-ORDINARY" OBSERVATION" WHEREBY THROUGH EXPIRIMENATION AND DEDUCTIVE REASONING ALONE, TO THE SPECIFIC EXCLUSION OF DIRECT SENSORY INPUTS, WE CAN UNDERSTAND THE TRUE NATURE OF THE EFFECTS THAT THE TRANSCENDENT DIMENSION HAS UPON ALL ELEMENTS THAT MANIFEST IN SPACE-TIME. STATED ALTERNATIVEY, THROUGH THIS OBSERVATION WE YET AGAIN REINFORCE THE UNIVESAL TRUTH THAT ALL THINGS IN THE UNIVERSE ARE HARDWIRED TOGETHER OR INTERCONNECTED, BUT WRAPPED IN A DECEIVING PARADOXICAL SEMI-PERMEABLE MEMBRANE.

C. Mathematical proof of Singularity in Paradox (Prove: ∞ = 1)

This section of the text is in its truest sense, is the principal foundation upon which the entirety of this text is built. Prior to constructing this proof the notion that all was one was a concept that was felt at depth. Further, the operations of quantum entanglement and the implications of the results of the 20th century modified versions of the double slit experiment proved satisfactory evidence supporting the truth that all is in fact one. It followed therefore that for this evidence to be conclusive its essence must be mathematically demonstrable. A mathematical proof must be constructible to validate this evidence. The equation is exceedingly simple:

$$\infty = 1$$

The construct of this proof had been exceedingly slippery and illusive. This in retrospect seemed to have been a function of its intrinsically paradoxical nature. To reiterate this paradox arises from the following:

1.) All is one;

2.) Existence requires more than one element;

3.) There is not more than one element

4.) The foregoing are mutually exclusive, yet both are true

5.) It follows therefore that the universe balances on Paradox

The path toward constructing this proof was frustrating. It was quite simple to quickly deduce that:

$$\infty = 0$$

This was accomplished by first reasoning that no mathematical operation can produce a result greater than ∞.

Following upon this, the following system of equations was developed:

$$\infty = \infty$$

$$100\infty = \infty$$

By applying a factor of -1 to the first equation, the following system results:

$$-\infty = -\infty$$

$$\underline{100\infty = \infty,}$$

$$99\,\infty = 0$$

$$\frac{99\ \infty}{99} = \frac{0}{99}$$

Solution: $\infty = 0$

The relatively obvious proof of $\infty = 0$ seemed counter intuitive. The objective was not to prove that $\infty = 0$, but to prove that $\infty = 1$. Following upon this analysis it became clear the proof was in fact designed to demonstrate the validity of paradox. The proof developed from that moment on as a clear rationalization of the paradox. Further, the elements of the proof do not hold true isolated within the four dimensions of space-time. The validity of the proof is limited to its application at the boundary of space-time and the transcendent, "non-local" or fifth dimension. For convenience, during the balance of this discussion it shall be referred to as the fifth dimension.

As it has been demonstrated here, $\infty = 0$. The implication of this half of the proof has value. As the paradox informs us, the infinite cannot exist outside of the paradoxical. Stated alternatively, something must create deception such that the infinite and interconnected nature of the fifth dimension experiences itself as a series of non-connected entities. To conclude, $\infty = 0$ informs us and reinforces the truth that the interconnected infinite can have no experiences and therefore does not exist and is at its essence nothing or zero absent Paradox.

This moves us to the second element of the proof. We mathematically demonstrated that $\infty = 0$, this reinforces one element of the paradox "One thing cannot have an experience, and therefore cannot exist".

If we want to demonstrate that $\infty = 1$; and we have shown that $\infty = 0$, it follows therefore, that if we can demonstrate that $0 = 1$, $\infty = 1$, by the transitive property of equality. It may be useful here to remind the reader that this is a proof whose validity is limited to the boundary between space-time and the transcendent dimension, for it is obvious that isolated inside space-time 0 does not equal 1.

This is similar in a converse manner to Einstein's Special Relativity being universally valid only within isolated space-time. It does not hold universally true outside the boundary of space-time.

The coordinate plane and infinite slopes have been used to demonstrate this half of the proof.

The following image shows a line that is nearly infinitely sloped:

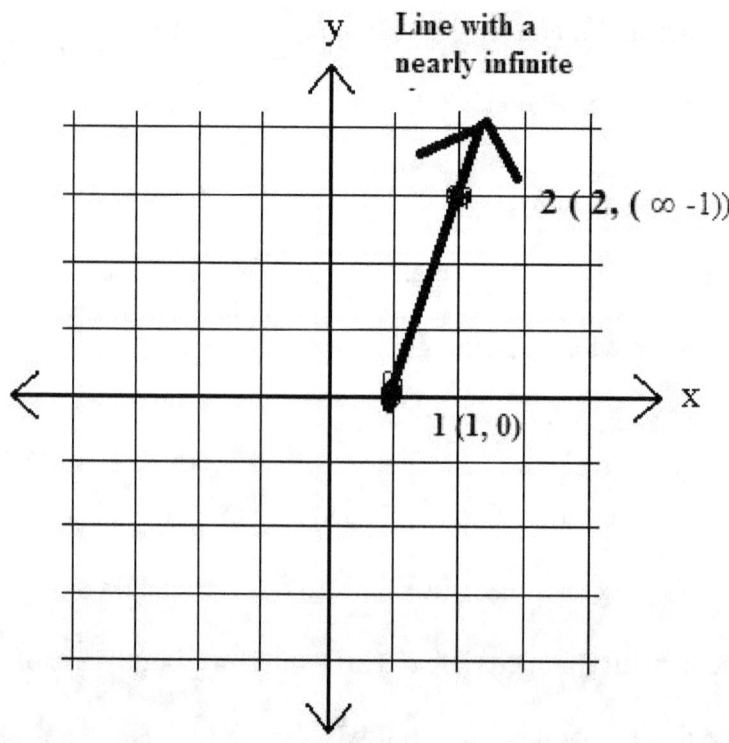

Let this line be Line 1

The slope of Line 1 =   change in y   =   ((∞-1) - 0)

change in x   (2 -1)

Slope of Line 1   = (∞-1)

Having thus calculated the slope of a line that is nearly infinitely

sloped, consider the following diagram of an infinitely sloped line

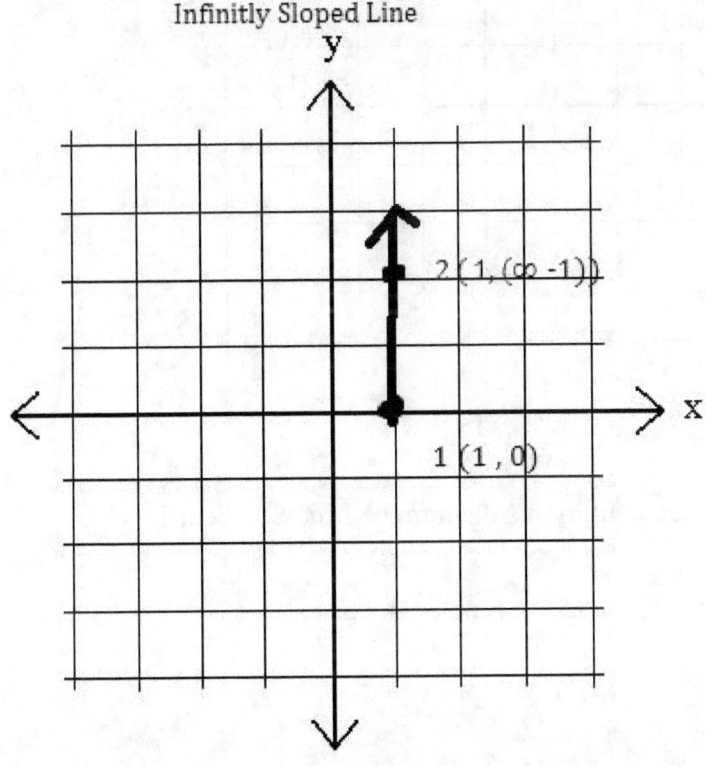

Let the Line in this diagram be Line 2

The slope of Line 2 > The slope of Line 1

The slope of Line 1 = Nearly Infinite

The slope of Line 2 is therefore infinite

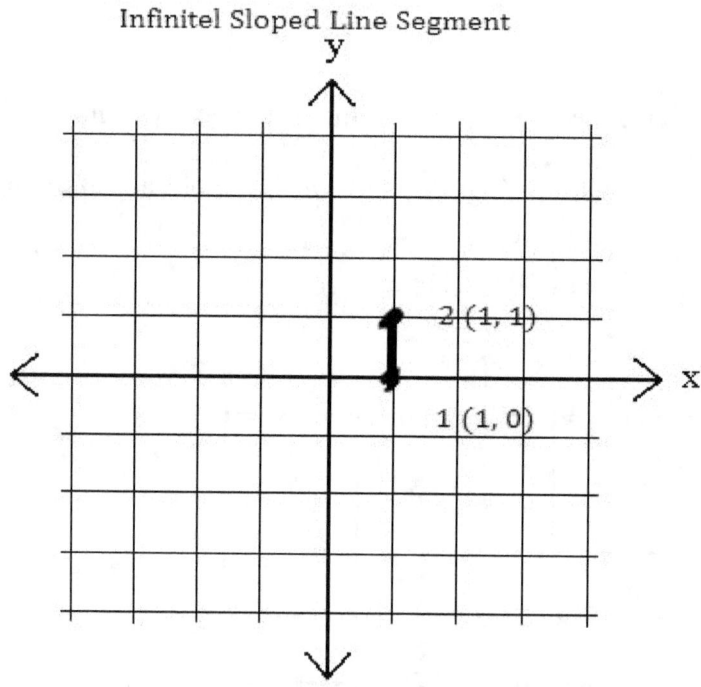

Infinitel Sloped Line Segment

Let the line segment in this diagram be Line Segment 1

Slope of Line 2 = Slope of Line Segment 1

Slope of Line 2 = ∞

Slope of Line Segment 1 = ∞

Slope of Line Segment 1 = ∞ = $\dfrac{\text{change y}}{\text{change x}}$ = $\dfrac{(1-0)}{(1-1)}$

$$\infty = \dfrac{1}{0}$$

Solution: 1 = 0

The summary of this half of the proof establishes that a line that has a greater slope than a line that is nearly infinite, is infinite. Further, that any segment of that infinitely sloped (vertical) line is also infinite. Therefore, the slope of the segment from (1,0) to (1,1), as the slope is infinite, set equal to its change in y over its change in x solves to 0 = 1. At this point it may be useful to reiterate that this proof validates an element of the paradox and is valid only at the barrier between space-time and the fifth dimension. Narratively, within this limitation 0 = 1, or 1 = 0. This half of the proof validates the precept within the paradox that the Oneness, or Singularity cannot exist, albeit paradoxically.

IT FOLLOWS THEREFORE, THAT AS $\infty = 0$ AND $0 = 1$;

TRANSITIVELY $\infty = 1$

VI. Emergence of Human Reasoning

A. Introduction

The purpose of this section of the text is constructed upon scriptural analytics as its principal method of gaining an understanding of truth. The allegory of the *Garden of Eden* will be deconstructed. In particular, the eating of the fruit from the *Tree of the Knowledge of Good and Evil*, the essence of Sin as inaccuracy, specifically an inaccuracy of understanding whose first result of death. Death as a function of sin and the Closing of Eden will be evaluated.

In the previous section we described three different means through which man is able to observe his universe in order to understand it and thereby function within it. The three methods are:

1.) Based upon his senses alone without deductive reasoning "Unreasoned Observation";

2.) Based upon his senses and deductive reasoning "Ordinary Observation" and

3.) Based upon his deductive reasoning alone "Non-Ordinary Observation'.

The *Eden* allegory tells the story of the birth of human reasoning capability. By being born into the ability to reason we can begin to expand our understanding of the universe and of truth. This however is the birth of reasoning, not its maturation. The process between the birth and maturation of reasoning is a time interval within the consciousness of man during which he cannot, through reason, see past the paradoxical barrier at the boundary of space-time and the transcendent *fifth dimension.*

Within this limitation, man's senses and limited reasoning ability lead him toward inaccurate conclusions about his own nature. The image of the fig leaf covering up shame is an image reinforcing the notion that born to reason, man observes himself as separated from the universe or if you prefer *The Fall*. He is seemingly disconnected and separated from other elements of the universe. In this state of separateness which is in contrast to a state of atonement he falsely observes that death is the ultimate outcome of life. This comes from "sinful" or inaccurate reasoning. The word "sin" etymologically speaking derives from archery. To "sin" literally means to miss the mark or the bullseye. In archery a sin lands on the target but not on the bulls-eye. While a miss misses the target entirely.

The "Fall of Man" as it is often referred to shall herein be posited to be a metaphor for the birth of reason which results in man's blindness to transcendent oneness. The maturational or gestational process of ordinary human reason or reasoning within the bounds of space-time into *Non-Ordinary* reasoning or reasoning that sees through the barrier between space-time and the transcendent dimension has been millennia in the making. During this time interval man's sinful or inaccurate understanding of truth has caused for him to construct systems, specifically social and economic systems, based upon his knowledge of the universe limited to Ordinary Observation. This specifically excludes the truths of interconnectivity which reside outside space-time. It is only possible to construct systems that harmonize resiliently if they are built on the truth of universal balance, harmony, abundance and interconnectivity. The systems of our current society, most notably our economic system is not constructed in such a manner. It is therefore out of harmony with truth. It therefore has and will **ALWAYS** produce chaotic results such as war, poverty and crime. It is clearly a sinful system in the most compelling and genuine meaning of the word.

B.   Fruit from the Tree of the Knowledge of Good and Evil

It seems useful to reiterate the purpose of this text often: *Its main purpose is to demonstrate beyond reasonable doubt that the universe is at its essence a singularity, an infinite interconnected field or if you prefer, the manifestation of an omnipotent and therefore omnipresent essence which operates through a paradoxical modality that transcends the boundary between the four-dimensions of space-time and the upper transcendent fifth dimension.*

In part, this shall be demonstrated by aligning this construct comparatively with the findings of quantum experimentation. As we have seen thus far, quantum experimentation discloses that a cohesion of all things exists outside of space-time. The ways of quantum entanglement provides clear evidence of this dynamic. To reinforce this newly emerging understanding of truth, the premise of the universe as a paradoxically unified singularity shall be tested against scriptural revelation. It seems exceedingly relevant and useful to compare the findings of quantum experimentation with ancient documents that have served man for millennia as a source from which he has sought an understanding of truth.

Those portions of the creation allegory set forth in Genesis 2 and 3 concerning the *Tree of the Knowledge of Good and Evil* prove a useful model of the emergence of human reasoning as a function of the paradoxically unified singularity which, as we have said before is synonymous with the word God, or alternatively still, the omnipotent and omnipresent essence of the paradoxically unified oneness. Consider the following excerpts:

> *"The LORD God made all kinds of trees grow out of the ground—trees that were pleasing to the eye and good for food. In the middle of the garden were the tree of life and the tree of the knowledge of good and evil."*
>
> *Genesis 2:9*
>
> *"And the LORD God commanded the man, "You are free to eat from any tree in the garden; but you must not eat from the tree of the knowledge of good and evil, for when you eat from it you will certainly die."*
>
> *Genesis 2:16-17*

"Adam and his wife were both naked, and they felt no shame"

Genesis 2:25

"Now the serpent was craftier than any of the wild animals the LORD God had made. He said to the woman, "Did God really say, 'You must not eat from any tree in the garden? The woman said to the serpent, "We may eat fruit from the trees in the garden, but God did say, you must not eat fruit from the tree that is in the middle of the garden [the Tree of the Knowledge of Good and Evil], and you must not touch it, or you will die. "You will not certainly die," the serpent said to the woman. "For God knows that when you eat from it your eyes will be opened, and you will be like God, knowing good and evil." When the woman saw that the fruit of the tree was good for food and pleasing to the eye, and also desirable for gaining wisdom, she took some and ate it. She also gave some to her husband, who was with her, and he ate it. Then the eyes of both of them were opened, and they realized they were naked; so they sewed fig leaves together and made coverings for themselves."

The name of the tree is revealing in itself: *"the Tree of the Knowledge of Good and Evil."* It seems quite clear that this reference aligns with the emergence of man's ability to reason, or stated alternatively, a new way of gaining understanding. Man was in that instance born into reason, yet his capacity for reason was highly limited. The text clearly states that when Adam and Eve ate the fruit *"the eyes of both of them were opened"*. Supporting the assertion that at that moment man was born into a capacity of sight that he had not previously possessed, or stated alternatively he was born into the capacity of reason. In Genesis 2:25, the last verse prior to the introduction of the serpent, it clearly states that Adam and Eve were both naked and felt no shame. Immediately upon the opening of their eyes they recognized their nakedness and were driven to cover themselves with sewn together fig leaves. Consider the timeline of the events as they illustrate the paradox:

1.) *"Adam and Eve were naked and felt no shame"*

   [ALL IS ONE]

2.) *"You will not certainly die,"* the serpent said to the

   woman. *"For God knows that when you eat from it*

your eyes will be opened, and you will be like God, KNOWING GOOD AND EVIL."

[DECEPTION / PARADOX]

3.) *"She saw that the fruit of the tree was good for food, pleasing to the eye and ALSO DESIRABLE FOR GAINING WISDOM"*

[INACCURATE UNDERSTANDING ("SIN")]

4.) *"...she took some and ate it. She also gave some to her husband who was with her and he ate it"*

[BEHAVIOR BASED UPON SIN]

5.) *"Then the eyes of both of them were opened"*

[BIRTH OF REASON]

6.) *"They recognized they were naked"*

[SHROUDING OF THE TRUTH OF ONENESS AS A FUNCTION OF PARADOX]

7.) *"They sewed fig leaves together and made coverings for themselves."*

[FALL FROM ATONED STATE]

Prior to the birth of reason, the events set forth above suggests man was in a state of grace or oneness with the universe, they "...*felt no shame*". Following the birth of reason "*they recognized they were naked...they sewed fig leaves together and made coverings for themselves".*

To summarize, the purpose of this section of the text is to reinforce the premise that the universe at its essence is an infinite cohesive field modulating paradoxically across a semi-permeable barrier between space-time and a transcendent *fifth dimension.* At this point we now introduce the birth of man's capacity to reason as a function of this universal paradox. The story of the *Fall told* in Genesis 2 and 3 illustrates that the birth of man's reasoning capacity is a direct function of paradox, metaphorically told through the words of *The Deceiver* (the "Serpent"). *The Deceiver, the Satanic or the Serpent,* are all synonymous with the paradoxical barrier between the four dimensions of space-time and the transcendent *fifth dimension.*

C.   Exploring the Paradox and Deception: The True Nature of Sin; Death as a Function of Sin.

To review, the universal paradox is restated here:

1.) All is one;

2.) Existence as a series of experiences or interactions requires more than one element;

3.) There is not more than one element

4.) The foregoing are mutually exclusive, yet both are true

5.) It follows therefore that the existence of the universe balances on Paradox

The construct that emerges from this Paradox is that of a barrier, boundary or separating force. Its operations seem something like a semi-permeable membrane that acts to separate the transcendent and universally interconnected *fifth dimension* from the four dimensions of space-time.

If we borrow from the Eden story, we can extract from the allegory that an event altered the way man observed the world:

"Then the eyes of both of them were opened, and they realized they were naked"

Genesis 3:7

At this point it is useful to relate Paradox and Deception. Regarding Quantum Entanglement, a seeming semi-permeable *"membrane"* between space-time and the *transcendent fifth dimension*, exists for the very purpose of facilitating existence to satisfy the logic of the Paradox. For the "Oneness" of the interconnected dimension to have experiences, it must manifest in space-time as seemingly separate elements. For as we have demonstrated and repeated here, without two elements there can be no experiences and therefore no existence. What is this construct but a form of deception?

The deceiver, the serpent or if you prefer the Satanic exists to deceive. The deception results in man being born into his reasoning ability. But prior to the emergence of Non-Ordinary Reasoning, man is blind to the presence of the Oneness of all things. Thereafter, man could only see the world from the limited perspective of "Self" as one of a series of disconnected elements. The first conclusion, based upon this deceived and inaccurate perspective is that his "self" is temporal and ceases to exist after an interval of time. Consider:

"For the wages of sin is death"

Romans 6:23

Out of context this verse of Romans suggests a punishing God. However, seen through the lens of Quantum Mechanics, interconnectivity and sin as blindness to universal oneness, it may become apparent that "Death" is a function of Sin, stated alternatively "Death" is a function of having been deceived. It follows that absent sin there is no death. As we evaluate this seemingly nonsensical statement we actually are able to validate its essence and follow it through to universal truth.

Consider that so far we have seen the similarity between Paradox and Deception. Outside of the paradoxical boundary of space-time "Everything is One". All things that manifest inside Space-time are projections of the infinite, interconnected, transcendent dimension, or the wave in quantum superposition. Following observation, the infinite wave collapses locally as particles which remain anchored in and connected through their non-local source in quantum superposition. Sin at its essence is blindness to oneness. Through this blindness to truth or "Sin" we cannot see through the paradoxical/deceptive barrier through to universal truth. We then move forward based upon a false perspective of ourselves and our relationship to the universe. In this instance the deception results in human consciousness being built upon a view that "I" is a distinguishable entity and not foundationally interconnected. This is clearly false. "I", operating as a function of this deception, or "sin", believes itself disconnected to the balance of the universe. In this perspective life is a function of time and therefore does not transcend it. It follows from this sinful or inaccurate perspective that death is inevitable. While to be certain, it is the nature of the universe that vessels, such as human bodies, are constructed to serve a purpose within the bounds of space-time. That purpose is to facilitate existence for a period of time and that at the end of that period the vessel will have outlived its effectiveness for this purpose. It is irrational however to then assert that this results in the end of the universe. While we see people who are given over to death, that is not the termination of existence for as we have said, demonstrated, repeated and reinforced that all is interconnected outside space-time and that the death of a body or a vessel is but a change and not an end. So indeed the wages of "sin" is death. To transcend death we need only look past our limited or "sinful" perspective on the universe which is a function of the universal deception and paradox, through to the truth of oneness. There is even a word for this process, which we have referred to and that word is "atonement", more specifically "atonement for sin". Stated alternatively, when instead of "sinning", I see past the deceptive and paradoxical nature of the universe, I see things accurately or non-sinfully. My sight, or stated alternatively, my ability to observe truth, is restored so that I see the oneness of all things. With my perspective corrected and adjusted to see my connection to the oneness of all things through the transcendent fifth dimension, I have overcome my "sinfulness" or my inaccuracy and again, without sin there is no death, it follows that as all things are one, death is thus transcended.

D.   The Closing of Eden

Consider the following excerpt:

To the woman he said:

I will make your pains in childbearing very severe; with painful labor you will give birth to children. Your desire will be for your husband, and he will rule over you."

To Adam he said,

"Because you listened to your wife and ate fruit from the tree about which I commanded you, 'You must not eat from it", Cursed is the ground because of you; through painful toil you will eat food from it all the days of your life. It will produce thorns and thistles for you, and you will eat the plants of the field. By the sweat of your brow you will eat your food until you return to the ground, since from it you were taken; for dust you are and to dust you will return."

Adam named his wife Eve because she would become the mother of all the living.

The LORD God made garments of skin for Adam and his wife and clothed them. And the LORD God said, "The man has now become like one of us, knowing good and evil. He must not be allowed to reach out his hand and take also from the tree of life and eat, and live forever." So the LORD God banished him from the Garden of Eden to work the ground from which he had been taken. After he drove the man out, he placed on the east side of the Garden of Eden cherubim and a flaming sword flashing back and forth to guard the way to the tree of life.

Genesis 16-24

We have explored the consistency of the ways of Quantum Mechanics through their paradoxical nature with the means through which human reasoning emerged as told metaphorically through the Eden Allegory. Following the closing of *Eden,* man is to toil and suffer. The conditions of his existence, born of sin or inaccuracy, molds his life as one lived in the shadow of death as a direct function of his inaccurate or gestational ability to reason, alternatively Sin. The placement of a flaming sword and a guarding cherubim provides an image of the paradoxical and deceptive barrier thus created between the mind of man and the ability to see the oneness of the universe. This is the birth of human society, from which social and economic systems emerged. As had been previously observed, all such systems, sinfully constructed, will never produce sustainably harmonious results. By broadening man's sight and ability to see through to the truth of oneness, a critical mass of men so empowered , can move toward replacing the socio-economic constructs of sin, death, scarcity, fear, poverty and war with newly enlightened constructs of harmony, abundance, life, oneness, prosperity and lasting peace. The birth of the internet provides the means through which this information can be rapidly disseminated.

VII. Characteristics of Gestational Human Reasoning

A.   Introduction

In the previous section, we explored the universal paradox which once again shall be restated here:

1.) All is one;

2.) Existence as a series of experiences or interactions requires more than one element;

3.) There is not more than one element

4.) The foregoing are mutually exclusive, yet both are true

5.) It follows therefore that the existence of the universe balances on Paradox

The forgoing paradox was compared and contrasted to the act of deception within the creation allegory set forth in Genesis 2 and 3. We saw an alignment in the allegory with this universal paradox. The barrier between space time and the transcendent *fifth dimension,* for the logic of the paradox to hold, must be maintained. The *Deceiving Serpent* of Genesis is analogous with the paradoxical barrier between space-time and the transcendent interconnected dimension. We saw how both the paradox and the

Satanic work toward creating a barrier between the lower world, or space time and the upper world or the *fifth dimension*. This semi-permeable membrane, as we had previously described it, seems to not only hold the boundary in Quantum Mechanics, it seems to also act to keep man's mind from finding its way back to a state of Atonement. Consider the following excerpt from the conclusion of the Eden allegory:

> *"The man has now become like one of us, knowing good and evil. He must not be allowed to reach out his hand and take also from the tree of life and eat, and live forever." So the* LORD *God banished him from the Garden of Eden to work the ground from which he had been taken. After he drove the man out, he placed on the east side of the Garden of Eden cherubim and a flaming sword flashing back and forth to guard the way to the tree of life.*

> *Genesis 3: 22-24*

We posited the alignment of the birth of human reason with Genesis' depiction of *The Fall*. The conclusion of Genesis 3 is the beginning of man's journey through the maturation of his reasoning capacity. During this time, the path back to Atonement through reason is metaphorically closed off to him the in the forms of guarding cherubim and a flaming sword. Further, he shall not be able to take from *The Tree of Life* and live forever. By referring to the *Tree of Life* in this context, the relationships between paradox, deception and universal interconnectivity, we can see how this closing off of man's access to the *Tree of Life,* is analogous to blinding him against seeing the transcendent dimension outside space-time, through which all things are manifestations of an eternal indestructible and interconnected field. With an inability to take from the *Tree of Life*, man is thus in a Fallen, Disconnected or Non-Atoned state. Believing disconnection to be true is thus sinful or inaccurate. The first result of this false perception or temporal scarcity is his belief in Death. Again all the days of his life are lived in the shadow of death, as the wages of this sinful or inaccurate perception.

This section shall provide a comparative of the relationship between Sin, Death and Economic scarcity. The fear making *666* shall be decoded as an extension of the concepts revealed through Quantum Experimentation and its alignment with gestational human reasoning. Additionally, the concepts of Economic Scarcity in the context of sinfulness, with a specific comparative analysis to Machiavelli's *The Prince*, shall be evaluated as the singular cause of war, poverty and crime. This section shall be concluded through a reinforcement of these concepts through a comparative analysis with ancient texts.

B. Sin, Death and Economic Scarcity

It is useful once again to reconnect the elements of the paradox to this section of text. The Paradox which emerges from observations in Quantum Experimentation represents the boundary between the infinite and interconnected, non-local, transcendent *fifth dimension* and the four-dimensions of space-time. The birth of man's reasoning capability, as metaphorically told in the allegory of *The Fall* (Genesis 2 and 3), illustrates the congruent nature of *The Deceiver or The Satanic* whose deception results in man's loss of an atoned state and that of the inter-dimensional boundary paradox.

As a result of *Original Sin,* man's consciousness is sealed off from the *Tree of Life* or the source which restores his natural, truthful, atoned and therefore timeless state. This illustrates the essence of sin which is the false perception of being in a disconnected or non-atoned state. As we had observed previously, per *Romans 6:23; "The Wages of Sin is Death"*. As we once again deconstruct that statement as we had in the previous section, we see that Death is a direct and dependent function of blindness to the true interconnected nature of the universe. This can be stated alternatively as our prohibition from "*Eating from the Fruit of the Tree of Life*", the *Universal Paradox or the Satanic Deception.*

Mans' development of reason has heretofore remained largely blind to this truth. Based upon his false perception of his own existence being a function of temporal scarcity he equates this with the dread of his prospective non-existence as the result of his death.

Mans' social system is at its essence an economic system. Consider that the means through which man sustains and safe guards himself are ALL economic in their nature. He cultivates food, he constructs shelter, and he secures land and water for his needs, among a broad range of other specific tasks. He falsely believes that time is scarce. From this starting point, with limited time, he extends this false belief to the quantity of resources he needs to sustain himself. How much time will it take to plant, to raise livestock, to purify drinking water and so on? Each of these tasks, based upon his blindness to the interconnectivity of all things, requires an allocation of his toil over the variable of finite time. He observes the systems that emerge from this process. He then concludes that the fruits of his work are a function of the finite quantity of time he has been allocated for existence. As we follow this through, the burdensome nature of his toil is such that it becomes desirable to free his limited time from toil so that it is available for ease and comfort. He equates his wellness as a condition describing his existence within the bounds of space-time as a function of the ability to secure an inexhaustible quantity of resources to sustain himself and maximize the utility of his time.

When man falsely believes in the notion of the scarcity of time, which as has been previously demonstrated is analogous with sin, he falsely believes his life is lived in the shadow of death. Upon this flawed perspective on truth, the resources, economic resources, he needs to continue to exist, are a clear function of toil over time. It follows then, as time if falsely perceived to be scarce, that economic resources must likewise as they are a function of time be scarce thusly. It is this dynamic which is both the foundational principal of all economic systems and by definition the cause of all economic discontinuity and disequilibrium. Further, these observations demonstrate incontrovertibly that the false or sinful perception of temporal and by extension economic scarcity is the direct and sole cause of war, greed, unsustainable wealth imbalances and poverty. Consider:

> *"Again I tell you, it is easier for a camel to go through the eye of a needle than for someone who is rich to enter the kingdom of God."*

Matthew 19:24

The kingdom of God can be seen from the perspective of a state of atonement. This is further reinforcement that the evidence of massive stored wealth in the possession of the wealthy is a clear function of a manner of living which is reflective of the deeply sinful and flawed perspective on reality that is rooted in the acceptance of the lie of temporal scarcity. In this modality, inner chaos, fear, deception and manipulation are those attributes which are maximally useful in the process of amassing wealth, they do not however produce a modality that has a high probability of resulting in atonement, inner harmony or a community of sustained peace amongst nations.

C. Marked as Beasts: *666* Decoded

"Let the person who has insight calculate the number of the beast,

for it is the number of a man. That number is 666."

Revelation 13:18

So far we have drawn connections between paradox and deception. We have drawn connections between the "hidden variable" outside of space time through which all things remain connected. We further have demonstrated that as a result of the birth of human reasoning, man has had his consciousness sealed off from the *Tree of Life,* or stated alternatively, sealed off from accessing the transcendent *fifth dimension.*

In this context, a singular man perceiving the lie of his disconnection is, dimensionally speaking, limited. Consider once again the observations of Einstein:

> *"A human being is a part of the whole called by us universe,*
> *a part limited in time and space. He experiences himself, his*
> *thoughts and feeling as something separated from the rest,*
> *a kind of optical delusion of his consciousness. This delusion*

is a kind of prison for us, restricting us to our personal desires and to affection for a few persons nearest to us. Our task must be to free ourselves from this prison by widening our circle of compassion to embrace all living creatures and the whole of nature in its beauty." (Einstein, A., Calaprice, A., (2005))

This excerpt of *Revelation* equates the number of the beast with the number of a man. It is very clear in that it refers to a single man. In the context of our exploration of the interdimensional ways of quantum mechanics and the allegorical exploration of Genesis, the notion of a man may indicate man as a function of sin and disconnection. The isolated and frightened "self". In this state, he is disconnected from the upper dimension, non-atoned. To borrow from Einstein *"He experiences his thoughts and feelings as something separated from the rest, a kind of optical delusion of consciousness. THIS DELUSION IS A KIND OF PRISON FOR US";* or alternatively *THIS DELUSIOON IS A KIND OF HELL FOR US.*

The visual 666, can be considered from the standpoint of the three dimensions of space, 6 by 6 by 6. Consciousness, fundamentally a fifth dimensional element, blind to its true nature which is interconnected and infinite is trapped within the Lower non-transcendent plane. In this mode, man's behavior more closely aligns to that of an unreasoned, frightened and therefoore potentially violent beast. Being trapped inside the 6x6x6 cube of space, ultimately man faces the impossibility or the limits of his reasoning as bound in the lower non-transcendent dimension. His reasoning and logic must fail as it is built upon *Paradox* or stated alternatively, *Satanic Deception.*

666 is an image of man's mind trapped outside of the ability to reason *five dimensionally*, as that ability requires access to the upper transcendent dimension to see truth, from which he is sealed off. Being thus trapped in a 6x6x6 prison of consciousness, he operates upon the scarcity of time, and follows this through to the notion of controlling and manipulating the behaviors of others to force them into his self-centered servitude as from the perspective of his flawed four-dimensional logical, he must secure inexhaustible material resources to assure his wellness within the shadow of deception and death. His behaviors in this manner produce the opposite of wellness, they produce disharmony, chaos, or if you prefer the impossibility of reason which has been described as *Hell.*

D. Machiavellian Ideals

Consider the following excerpt from Chapter 17 of Machiavelli's *The Prince:*

> *... I say that every Prince should desire to be accounted merciful and not cruel. Nevertheless, he should be on his guard against the abuse of this quality of mercy. Cesare Borgia was reputed cruel, yet his cruelty restored Romagna, united it, and brought it to order and obedience; so that if we look at things in their true light, it will be seen that he was in reality far more merciful than the people of Florence, who, to avoid the imputation of cruelty, suffered Pistoja to be torn to pieces by factions.*
>
> *A Prince should therefore disregard the reproach of being thought cruel where it enables him to keep his subjects united and obedient. For he who quells disorder by a very few signal examples will in the end be more merciful than he who from too great leniency permits things to take their course and so to result in rapine and bloodshed; for these hurt the whole State, whereas the severities of the Prince injure individuals only...*

...And here comes in the question whether it is better to be loved rather than feared, or feared rather than loved. It might perhaps be answered that we should wish to be both; but since love and fear can hardly exist together, if we must choose between them, it is far safer to be feared than loved. For of men it may generally be affirmed, that they are thankless, fickle, false, studious to avoid danger, greedy of gain, devoted to you while you are able to confer benefits upon them, and ready, as I said before, while danger is distant, to shed their blood, and sacrifice their property, their lives, and their children for you; but in the hour of need they turn against you. The Prince, therefore, who without otherwise securing himself builds wholly on their professions is undone. For the friendships which we buy with a price, and do not gain by greatness and nobility of character, though they be fairly earned are not made good, but fail us when we have occasion to use them.

In the text thus far we have connected the notions of *Satanic Deception and Paradox*. Further we have drawn parallels between the reality of the universe being composed of the four-dimensions of space-time and a "Non-local" transcendent dimension which operates, as evidenced by the results of quantum experimentation, as an infinite, interconnected wave in quantum superposition, and the allegory of *The Fall,* as told in Genesis 2 and 3 which describes the results of the universal paradox or the Satanic Deception causing man to be sealed off from the ability to see the universal truth of interconnectivity. Being thus blinded, he loses sight of truth and is therefore errant (sinful), and born to the false belief in the validity of temporal scarcity and death.

Upon these connections, the previous section explored the notion of the false perception of temporal scarcity. This results in the false perception of the scarcity of economic resources as they are a function of time. As these notions are untrue, and the proof of their falsehood has been sealed off from man's mind through the universal Paradox, He has built economic systems that have not and will never produce sustainable harmony, because their founding principal is scarcity which is invalid. Set in the context of these observations, Machiavelli's *The Prince,* gives an excellent view of the mindset from which our society has been ordered. As Machiavelli rightly points out, blinded from the ability to see past the Paradoxical or Satanic barrier through to the truth of interconnectivity:

> ...*it may generally be affirmed [of men], that they are thankless, fickle, false, studious to avoid danger, greedy of gain...*

The sovereign (or state) has long been ordered upon this perspective. Later in the text, we will discuss the beginnings of the notions of John Locke regarding Natural Law, the Equality of All Men and the righteousness of any social or governmental form arising only through a consent of the people. Regardless, from the time of Eden, through Machiavelli, past Locke to the United States Constitution, our socio-economic constructs remain firmly built upon the false and broken notion of temporal and economic scarcity. Upon these notions man is indeed thankless, fickle and greedy, it follows therefore that our socio-economic constructs will continue to breed war and poverty until they are reset upon the truth of abundance and harmony, instead of the satanic and paradoxical deceptions of scarcity, fear, want, death, war and poverty.

E. Economic Evaluation of Scripture

Thus far we have demonstrated, through an exploration of: 1.) the results of quantum experimentation and 2.) *The Fall* as allegorically told in Genesis 2 and 3, the validity of the Oneness of all things through the reality of an upper dimension residing "non-locally" in quantum superstition outside space-time, or stated alternatively the *Tree of Life,* from which man's eternal nature originates and continues.

By extension, we have posited and explored the notion, that having been blinded to universal interconnectivity as a function of existential Paradox, or stated alternatively *Satanic Deception,* man's mind is built upon the false perception of temporal scarcity. Next, as the cultivation of economic resource are a function of time, (toil over time), and man deeply accepts the lie of temporal scarcity (death), he operates in a manner reflective of this false perception that as time is scarce and economic resources are a function of time, that it follows that economic resources are scarce thusly. To reiterate however, the notion of temporal scarcity is fundamentally untrue, therefore the logic process which extends this notion of temporal scarcity to scarcity of economic resources is unequivocally flawed and therefore misleading.

These observations and connections shall be further reinforced and supported through an evaluation of the following sources:

i.   *James 5: 1 – 6. "WARNING TO RICH OPPRESSORS"*

"Now listen, you rich people, weep and wail because of the misery that is coming on you. Your wealth has rotted, and moths have eaten your clothes. Your gold and silver are corroded. Their corrosion will testify against you and eat your flesh like fire. You have hoarded wealth in the last days. Look! The wages you failed to pay the workers who mowed your fields are crying out against you. The cries of the harvesters have reached the ears of the Lord Almighty. You have lived on earth in luxury and self-indulgence. You have fattened yourselves in the day of slaughter. You have condemned and murdered the innocent one, who was not opposing you.

In a future section of this text the wealth disparity as it exist within the United States of the early 21st century will be evaluated to demonstrate its root as a function of the paradoxical and satanic, as these concepts have been developed throughout this text. This excerpt of *James,* clearly describes hoarded wealth as evidence of a sinful or blinded mindset. It further makes clear that gold and silver, as symbols of hoarded wealth will be revealed to be no effective source of peace and relief for its possessors. The economic injustices that were engaged in, the withholding of equitable compensation for the toil of workers, which gave rise to their possession of the stored gold and silver will be adjusted for as manifest in the weeping and wailing of the rich. Their suffering is a direct function of their orientation towards deception whose end is hoarding of material wealth which they falsely believe will mute the sting of toil, scarcity and death. The only source of relief from the suffering which is born of the false notions of temporal scarcity (death), is the light of truth which shines to illuminate the path back to the healing and harmonizing of interconnectivity (atonement), and the falsehood of temporal and economic scarcity.

ii.   *Deuteronomy   5:   8   –   10.   "THE   SECOND*
COMMANDMENT"

"You shall not make for yourself an image in the form of
anything in heaven above or on the earth beneath or in
the waters below. You shall not bow down to them or
worship them; for I, the LORD your God, am a jealous
God, punishing the children for the sin of the parents to
the third and fourth generation of those who hate me, but
showing love to a thousand generations of those who
love me and keep my commandments."

Once again, the second commandment guides that the process of
creating false idols, such as stored wealth is prohibited. This
process is clearly analogous to the sinful or blind thinking that
equates the possession of stored material wealth with security,
calm of heart and well-being. Security, calm of heart and well-
being are functions of being atoned with universal truth. The
hoarding of wealth is a function of sin, deception and its resultant
fear of the lie of death. The effects that follow, is that children of
such sin, as hoarded wealth carries through generationally to the
third and fourth generation, suffer the same blindness and sinful

mindset. They grow accustomed to the process of wealth being a means through which they have power over others, reinforcing the lie of separation and differentiation and more deeply constructing the paradoxical and satanic barrier between their minds and hearts and the upper dimension of interconnectivity, selflessness, joy in the service of others and true harmony, universal brotherhood security and peace.

iii. Ecclesiastes 5: 8 – 12: "RICHES ARE MEANINGLESS"

"If you see the poor oppressed in a district, and justice and rights denied, do not be surprised at such things; for one official is eyed by a higher one, and over them both are others higher still. The increase from the land is taken by all; the king himself profits from the fields."

"Whoever loves money never has enough; whoever loves wealth is never satisfied with their income. This too is meaningless. As goods increase, so do those who consume them. And what benefit are they to the owners except to feast their eyes on them? The sleep of a laborer is sweet, whether they eat little or much, but as for the rich, their abundance permits them no sleep."

Ecclesiastes, the laments of Solomon the great king, born and raised in wealth all the days of his life, gained great wisdom and the capacity for self-reflection. From within the bounds of the prison of his own wealth, he recognized its intergenerational toxicity. *Whoever loves money never has enough.* But why is this so? In the context of trans-dimensional cohesion and interconnectivity, we can observe that blindness and sinfulness as a function of the paradox or the satanic, creates the false perception of temporal scarcity. Temporal scarcity, being falsely received as true, results in the notion that money, as it inequitably harvests the value of the toil/time of others through their forced servitude, will never deaden the specter of temporal scarcity or death. It is only through harmonizing with the truth of interconnectivity or atonement that one can be freed of the hell of temporal scarcity. The rich have no peace as they do not serve, they deceive and compel others to serve them. Conversely the sleep of the laborer is sweet (i.e. at peace) as his act of service harmonizes with the truth of interconnectivity.

iv. Revelations 18

a. *"LAMENT OVER FALLEN BABYLON". After this I saw another angel coming down from heaven. He had great authority, and the earth was illuminated by his splendor. With a mighty voice he shouted: "Fallen! Fallen is Babylon the Great! "She has become a dwelling for demons and a haunt for every impure spirit, a haunt for every unclean bird, a haunt for every unclean and detestable animal. For all the nations have drunk the maddening wine of her adulteries. The kings of the earth committed adultery with her, and the merchants of the earth grew rich from her excessive luxuries."*

b. *WARNING TO ESCAPE BABYLON'S JUDGEMENT: "Then I heard another voice from heaven say: "Come out of her, my people, so that you will not share in her sins, so that you will not receive any of her plagues; for her sins are piled up to heaven, and God has remembered her crimes. Give back to her as she has given; pay her back double for what she has done. Pour her a double portion from her own cup. Give her as much torment and grief as the glory and luxury she gave herself. In her heart she boasts, 'I sit enthroned as queen. I am not a widow; I will never mourn.' Therefore in one day her plagues will overtake her: death, mourning and famine. She will be consumed by fire, for mighty is the Lord God who judges her.*

c. *THREEFOLD WOE OVER BABYLON'S FALL.* "When the kings of the earth who committed adultery with her and shared her luxury see the smoke of her burning, they will weep and mourn over her. Terrified at her torment, they will stand far off and cry: "Woe! Woe to you, great city, you mighty city of Babylon! In one hour your doom has come!". "The merchants of the earth will weep and mourn over her because no one buys their cargoes anymore cargoes of gold, silver, *precious stones and pearls; fine linen, purple, silk and scarlet, cloth; every sort of citron wood, and articles of every kind made of ivory, costly wood, bronze, iron and marble; cargoes of cinnamon and spice, of incense, myrrh and frankincense, of wine and olive oil, of fine flour and wheat; cattle and sheep; horses and carriages; and human beings sold as slaves. They will say, 'The fruit you longed for is gone from you. All your luxury and splendor have vanished, never to be recovered.' The merchants who sold these things and gained their wealth from her will stand far off, terrified at her torment. They will weep and mourn and cry out: "'Woe! Woe to you, great city, dressed in fine linen, purple and scarlet, and glittering with gold, precious stones and pearls! In one hour such great wealth has been brought to ruin!' "Every sea captain, and all who travel by ship, the sailors, and all who earn their living from the sea, will stand far off. When they see the smoke of her burning, they will exclaim, 'Was there ever a city like this great city?' They will throw dust on their heads, and with weeping and mourning cry out:" 'Woe! Woe to you, great city, where all who had ships on the sea became rich through her wealth! In one hour she has been brought to ruin!' "Rejoice over her, you heavens! Rejoice, you people of God! Rejoice, apostles and prophets! For God has judged her with the judgment she imposed on you."*

d. *THE FINALITY OF BABYLON'S DOOM Then a mighty angel picked up a boulder the size of a large millstone and threw it into the sea, and said: "With such violence the great city of Babylon will be thrown down, never to be found again. The music of harpists and musicians, pipers and trumpeters, will never be heard in you again. No worker of any trade will ever be found in you again. The sound of a millstone*

will never be heard in you again. The light of a
lamp will never shine in you again. The voice
of bridegroom and bride will never be heard in
you again. Your merchants were the world's
important people. By your magic spell all the
nations were led astray. In her was found the
blood of prophets and of God's holy people, of
all who have been slaughtered on the earth."

In *Revelation 18* we clearly see intense suffering arise from what is essentially corruption of the state through which economic injustices are facilitated. It is a recurrent theme, that man, blinded through *Original Sin, Paradox or Satanic Deception*, is prone to repeatedly construct social systems of kings and merchants and powerful men, who prove most adept in the types of economic deception that lead to copious stored wealth. The drive for stored wealth is a direct function of delusion. That delusion is the belief in the lie of temporal scarcity. It is little wonder then that the wealthiest and most powerful within a sinfully constructed socio-economic paradigm will largely be those with the thickest blindness from truth and the greatest capacity for deception.

"For the love of money is a root of all kinds of evil. Some people, eager for money, have wandered from the faith and pierced themselves with many griefs."

Yet again, love of money as the root of many evils. The love of money, as we have seen evidences a sinful or deceived mindset. Blindness to the lie of temporal scarcity, manifests in the mind of man as economic scarcity. It logically follows, albeit upon false premise, that the hoarding of wealth will result is a sense of wellness. The process of hoarding greater and greater stores of wealth are always a function of deception and coercion, such that the hoarder of wealth harvests the fruits of the laborers' toil, and in so doing the hoarder becomes an agent of deception or evil.

    vi.   Allegory of the Cave *(Plato's Republic)*

      Consider the following excerpts:

..."Behold! Human beings live in an underground den, which has a mouth open towards the light and reaching all along the den. Here they have been from their childhood, and

have their legs and necks chained so that they cannot move, and can only see before them, being prevented by the chains from turning round their heads. Above and behind them a fire is blazing at a distance, and between the fire and the prisoners there is a raised way; and you will see, if you look, a low wall built along the way, like the screen which marionette players have in front of them, over which they show the puppets."

.... "And now look again, and see what will naturally follow if the prisoners are released and disabused of their error. At first, when any of them is liberated and compelled suddenly to stand up and turn his neck round and walk and look towards the light, he will suffer sharp pains; the glare will distress him, and he will be unable to see the realities of which in his former state he had seen the shadows; and then conceive someone saying to him, that what he saw before was an illusion, but that now, when he is approaching nearer to being and his eye is turned towards more real existence, he has a clearer vision, what will be his reply ? And you may further imagine that his instructor

130

is pointing to the objects as they pass and requiring him to name them, will he not be perplexed? Will he not fancy that the shadows which he formerly saw are truer than the objects which are now shown to him?"

... *"And suppose once more, that he is reluctantly dragged up a steep and rugged ascent, and held fast until he's forced into the presence of the sun himself, is he not likely to be pained and irritated? When he approaches the light his eyes will be dazzled, and he will not be able to see anything at all of what are now called 'realities'"*

..... *"He will then proceed to argue that this is he who gives the season and the years, and is the guardian of all that is in the visible world, and in a certain way the cause of all things which he and his fellows have been accustomed to behold?"... "And when he remembered his old habitation, and the wisdom of the den and his fellow-prisoners, do you not suppose that he would felicitate himself on the change, and pity them?"... "It is the task of the enlightened not only to ascend to learning and to see the good but to be willing to*

131

descend again to those prisoners and to share their troubles and their honors, whether they are worth having or not. And this they must do, even with the prospect of death."

... "And if they were in the habit of conferring honors among themselves on those who were quickest to observe the passing shadows and to remark which of them went before, and which followed after, and which were together; and who were therefore best able to draw conclusions as to the future, do you think that he would care for such honors and glories, or envy the possessors of them? Would he not say with Homer "Better to be the poor servant of a poor master, and to endure anything, rather than think as they do and live after their manner?"

..."Imagine once more", I said, "such a one coming suddenly out of the sun to be replaced in his old situation; would he not be certain to have his eyes full of darkness?"

...*"And if there were a contest, and he had to compete in measuring the shadows with the prisoners who had never moved out of the den, while his sight was still weak, and before his eyes had become steady (and the time which would be needed to acquire this new habit of sight might be very considerable) would he not be ridiculous? Men would say of him that up he went and down he came without his eyes; and that it was better not even to think of ascending; and if any one tried to lose another and lead him up to the light, let them only catch the offender, and they would put him to death".*

... the prison house is the world of sight, the light of the fire is the sun, and you will not misapprehend me if you interpret the journey upwards to be the ascent of the soul into the intellectual world according to my poor belief, which, at your desire, I have expressed -- whether rightly or wrongly God knows. But, whether true or false, my opinion is that in the world of knowledge the idea of good appears last of all, and is seen only with an effort; and, when seen, is also inferred to be the universal author of all

133

things beautiful and right, parent of light and of the lord of light in this visible world, and the immediate source of reason and truth in the intellectual; and that this is the power upon which he who would act rationally, either in public or private life must have his eye fixed".

..."you must not wonder that those who attain to this beatific vision are unwilling to descend to human affairs; for their souls are ever hastening into the upper world where they desire to dwell; which desire of theirs is very natural, if our allegory may be trusted".

..."Whereas, our argument shows that the power and capacity of learning exists in the soul already; and that just as the eye was unable to turn from darkness to light without the whole body, so too the instrument of knowledge can only by the movement of the whole soul be turned from the world of becoming into that of being, or in other words, of the good".

..."And whereas the other so-called virtues of the soul seem to be akin to bodily qualities, for even when they are not originally innate they can be implanted later by habit and exercise, the virtue of wisdom more than anything else contains a divine element which always remains, and by this conversion is rendered useful and profitable; or, on the other hand, hurtful and useless. Did you never observe the narrow intelligence flashing from the keen eye of a clever rogue? How eager he is, how clearly his paltry soul sees the way to his end? He is the reverse of blind, but his keen eye-sight is forced into the service of evil, and he is mischievous in proportion to his cleverness".

..."Yes", I said; "and there is another thing which is likely, or rather a necessary inference from what has preceded, that neither the uneducated and uninformed of the truth, nor yet those who never make and end of their education, will be able ministers of State; not the former, because they have no single aim of duty which is the rule of all their actions, private as well as public; nor the latter, because they will not act at all except upon compulsion, fancying *that they are already dwelling apart in the Islands of the Blest".*

..."I mean that they remain in the upper world: but this must not be allowed; they must be made to descend again among the prisoners in the den, and partake of their labors and honors, whether they are worth having or not"

..." there will be no injustice in compelling our philosophers to have a care and providence of others; we shall explain to them that in other States, men of their class are not obliged to share in the toils of politics: and this is reasonable, for they grow up at their own sweet will, and the government would rather not have them. Being self-taught, they cannot be expected to show any gratitude for a culture which they have never received. But we have brought you into the world to be rulers of the hive, kings of yourselves and of the other citizens, and have educated you far better and more perfectly than they have been educated, and you are better able to share in the double duty. Wherefore each of you, when his turn comes, must go

down to the general underground abode, and get the habit of seeing in the dark. When you have acquired the habit, you will see ten thousand times better than the inhabitants of the den, and you will know what the several images are, and what they represent, because you have seen the beautiful and just and good in their truth. And thus our State which is also yours will be a reality, and not a dream only, and will be administered in a spirit unlike that of other States, in which men fight with one another about shadows only and are distracted in the struggle for power, which in their eyes is a great good. Whereas the truth is that the State in which the rulers are most reluctant to govern is always the best and most quietly governed, and the State in which they are most eager, the worst".

..."and there lies the point. You must contrive for your future rulers another and a better life than that of a ruler, and then you may have a well-ordered State; for only in the State which offers this, will they rule who are truly rich, not in silver and gold, but in virtue and wisdom, which are the true blessings of life. Whereas if they go to the *administration of public affairs, poor and hungering after their own private advantage, thinking that hence they are to snatch the chief good, order there can never be; for they will be fighting about office, and the civil and domestic broils which thus arise will be the ruin of the rulers themselves and of the whole State".*

The allegory of the cave provides very clear foundation for the upper dimension. This is a place in which man can ascend and see truth. However, born in the cave he is born to darkness and grows accustomed to equate the observed shadows within the lower world of the cave with the limits of truth. Socrates is quick to inform us of the economic implications which are a function of the limited sight of those in the prison of the cave *"Did you never observe the narrow intelligence flashing from the keen eye of a clever rogue? How eager he is, how clearly his paltry soul sees the way to his end? He is the reverse of blind, but his keen eye-sight is forced into the service of evil, and he is mischievous in proportion to his cleverness".* He observes further that: [the State] *in which men fight with one another about shadows only and are distracted in the struggle for power, which in their eyes is a great good".* The shadows Socrates refers to are the separate economic resources of the State constructed by those blind to the truth of the upper world. Again further reference to the truth that economic systems born in the darkness of the cave, constructed blind to the presence of the existential paradox or subject to Satanic perception, will never take the form of *The Republic* he recommends he and his students endeavor to be the founders of, one based upon sight and understanding of the presence of the upper world, or stated alternatively, transcendent of the existential paradox, or a gaze which overcomes Satanic Deception.

vii.   *John 15: 18-25 "THE WORLD HATES THE DISCIPLES"; and John 16: 1-4*

> *...If the world hates you, keep in mind that it hated me first. If you belonged to the world, it would love you as its own. As it is, you do not belong to the world, but I have chosen you out of the world. That is why the world hates you. Remember what I told you: 'A servant is not greater than his master. If they persecuted me, they will persecute you also. If they obeyed my teaching, they will obey yours also. They will treat you this way because of my name, for they do not know the one who sent me. If I had not come and spoken to them, they would not be guilty of sin; but now*

they have no excuse for their sin. Whoever hates me hates my Father as well. If I had not done among them the works no one else did, they would not be guilty of sin. As it is, they have seen, and yet they have hated both me and my Father. But this is to fulfill what is written in their Law: 'They hated me without reason.

... "All this I have told you so that you will not fall away. They will put you out of the synagogue; in fact, the time is coming when anyone who kills you will think they are offering a service to God. They will do such things because they have not known the Father or me. I have told you this, so that when their time comes you will remember that I warned you about them. I did not tell you this from the beginning because I was with you"

Here, Christ describes for his followers: that as they have been born into the sight of truth, within the bounds of their dark lower world of highly limited enlightenment, they will experience rejection, persecution, torture and death at the hands of the authorities of the lower world, the Princes of the Lower World, the Princes of Deception. Christ's teachings in this context directly align with those in the *Allegory of the Cave*.

F.   Conclusion

The purpose of this section is to reinforce the relationships between what has become known through quantum experimentation, namely the presence of a dimension which transcends space-time through which all things are interconnected with the observations of ancient texts pointing toward the very same universal truth. Further, in both quantum experimentation and in scripture, deception and paradox are central. As we have said before, the natural state of the universe is that of an interconnected singularity or oneness wrapped in paradox or deception, such that the false perception of plurality is conjured in order to facilitate interaction and thus existence.

It follows upon this that the essence of cohesion or oneness was "sealed up" from man's sight. Blinded to oneness, man's consciousness is: *Fallen, Non-Atoned, Paradoxical or Satanically Deceived.* In this modality, the false belief in the separate or disconnected nature of man's essence causes him to then falsely observe the nature of time. In this false manner he observes that the time for existence is scarce. This sinful perspective gives rise to death, as death is a function of scarce time. As we have demonstrated however, time is eternal and not scarce, it follows therefore that death is an illusion.

Regardless, however, the effectiveness of the Paradox or the Satanic Deception is formidable. So much so that man has remained in this prison of his delusional consciousness for millennia.

Man operates at the root of his consciousness upon the deception of temporal scarcity. He observes that the economic resources, expressed as the function of toil over time, are a function of the scarce element of time. It follows then, that he accept the errant conclusion that economic resources are scarce. This precept has ordered social, economic and governmental constructs throughout history.

Repeatedly, this system descends into greater and greater corruption as a function of the continuation of man's blindness to interconnected truth. He therefore, desperately attempts to alleviate the suffering which arises from this inner disharmony by hoarding economic resources. As man falsely and subconsciously perceives his woes to be a function of temporal scarcity, he subconsciously reasons that by harvesting the time of others (the effect of wealth hoarding) he delusionaly believes he can arrive at a destination of inner peace, contentment, security and happiness. Reality however, is that these efforts produce the opposite effect. The only source of inner peace is an alignment with the infinite and universal truth of oneness. The process of hoarding and using wealth is a function of deception. His inner discord rises as the barrier of the paradox and satanic between the wealth hoarding agent of deception and the source of truth thickens as a direct function of his own acts of manipulation, forced servitude and deception.

References:

Einstein, A., Calaprice, A., & Einstein, A. (2005). *The new quotable Einstein*. Princeton, N.J: Princeton University Press.

VIII.   Birth and expansions of Enlightenment and Revolution

A.   Introduction

The purpose of this section is to explore the effects that the technology of information distribution has had on facilitating man's ability to see through to genuine truth and begin the long process of transcending the limitations of the socio-economic hell he has constructed as a function of his limited sight and reasoning ability. The 21st Century is the time during which man shall free himself from his imprisonment from this darkness. We shall observe that the central and lasting effect of man's first shift in information distribution, the printing press, resulted in the adoption of *Governmental Systems* based upon the emergence of man's ability to see the truthfulness of *Natural Law*. And that only upon the truth of *Natural Law* can any righteous form of *Government* be established. The evidence of the past 300 years clearly demonstrates that a *Governmental* construct built upon *Natural Law* is of limited beneficial effect if global economic systems remain firmly built upon the deception of scarcity. In this section we shall explore the effect that the printed word has had upon the expansion of enlightenment which in turn has effected man's drive to restructure his world based upon his broadened gaze upon the truth of universal oneness.

B. Printing Press

Cause and effect. It seems impossible to escape the conclusion that Gutenberg's impact on the development and wide spread use of the printing press in approximately 1440 incubated and facilitated the Protestant Reformation, the birth of the Scientific Revolution and the Enlightenment. At the essence of each of these developments is rapid and broad communication of ideas through the printed word. There is however, surprisingly scarce analysis which directly explores the cause and effect relationship of the printing press and the rapid spread of the ideas of Luther, Copernicus, Galileo, Newton, Bacon, and Locke. It seems *Self-Evident,* that the refinement of the reforms and observations of Luther and Copernicus, which blaze trail for the great thinkers of the Enlightenment, have at their root the Printing Press as a vessel to efficiently convey thoughts and guide a deep questioning of universal constructs and truths. Culminating in Locke's observations on *Natural Law.*

To reinforce these connections, consider the following observations from the introduction to *Five Centuries of Printing (Steinberg & Trevitt, 1996):*

Discourse was deemed man's noblest attribute,

And written words the glory of his hand.

Then followed printing with enlarged command

For Thought – dominion vast and absolute

For spreading truth and making love expand.

Wordsworth

"The history of printing is an integral part of the general history of civilization. The principal vehicle for the conveyance of ideas during the past five hundred years, printing touches on, and often penetrates, almost every sphere of human activity. Neither political, constitutional, ecclesiastical and economic events, nor sociological, philosophical and literary movements can be fully understood without taking into account the influence which the printing press has exerted on them."

The printing press sparked a tremendous increase in the quantity of information people could gain access to. It seems no coincidence that the ability to distribute, expand and explore foundational truths would find application as it had with the ideas of religious freedoms and reformation as well as ideas concerning the equality amongst all men and that righteous governmental systems can only arise upon these fundamental principles. These ideas are set forth clearly in Locke's *Two Treatises of Government,* which supported the notion of representative government both in England following The Glorious Revolution, and became the philosophical undercurrent of the form of Government established in the United States.

C.   Locke and Natural Law

In *Two Treatises on Government* Locke provides an underwriting of Natural Law as the only righteous basis upon which a sustainable and harmonious Governmental Construct can be established. Consider the following excerpts:

> *"This equality of men by nature, the judicious Hooker looks upon as so evident in itself, and beyond all question, that he makes it the foundation of that obligation to mutual love amongst men, on which he builds the duties we owe one another, and from whence he derives the great maxims of justice and charity. His words are,*

> *"The like natural inducement hath brought men to know, that it is no less their duty to love others than themselves; for seeing those things which are equal, must needs all have one measure; if I cannot but wish to receive good, even as much at every man's hands, as any man can wish unto his own soul, how should I look to have any part of my desire herein satisfied, unless myself be careful to satisfy the like desire, which is undoubtedly in other men, being of one and the same nature? To have anything*

150

offered them repugnant to this desire, must needs in all respects grieve them as much as me; so that if I do harm, I must look to suffer, there being no reason that others should show greater measure of love to me, than they have by me showed unto them: my desire therefore to be loved of my equals in nature, as much as possibly may be, imposeth upon me a natural duty of bearing to them-ward fully the like affection: from which relation of equality between ourselves and them that are as ourselves, what several rules and canons natural reason hath drawn, for direction of life, no man is ignorant."

"But though this be a state of liberty, yet it is not a state of license: though man in that state have an uncontrollable liberty to dispose of his person or possessions, yet he has not liberty to destroy himself, or so much as any creature in his possession, but where some nobler use than its bare preservation calls for it. The state of nature has a law of nature to govern it, which obliges every one: and reason, which is that law, teaches all mankind, who will but consult it, that being all equal and independent, no one

ought to harm another in his life, health, liberty, or possessions: for men being all the workmanship of one omnipotent and infinitely wise Maker; all the servants of one sovereign master, sent into the world by his order, and about his business; they are his property, whose workmanship they are, made to last during his, not another's pleasure: and being furnished with like faculties, sharing all in one community of nature, there cannot be supposed any such subordination among us, that may authorize us to destroy another, as if we were made for one another's uses, as the inferior ranks of creatures are for ours. Every one, as he is bound to preserve himself, and not to quit his station willfully, so by the like reason, when his own preservation comes not in competition, ought he, as much as he can, to preserve the rest of mankind, and may not, unless it be to do justice to an offender, take away or impair the life, or what tends to the preservation of life, the liberty, health, limb, or goods of another."

"And that all men may be restrained from invading others rights, and from doing hurt to one another, and the law of

nature be observed, which willeth the peace and preservation of all mankind, the execution of the law of nature is, in that state, put into every man's hands, whereby everyone has a right to punish the transgressors of that law to such a degree as may hinder its violation: for the law of nature would, as all other laws that concern men in this world, be in vain, if there were nobody that in the state of nature had a power to execute that law, and thereby preserve the innocent and restrain offenders. And if anyone in the state of nature may punish another for any evil he has done, every one may do so: for in that state of perfect equality, where naturally there is no superiority or jurisdiction of one over another, what any may do in prosecution of that law, everyone must needs have a right to do."

In the preceding excerpts, we discover Locke's basis for constructing Governmental systems upon natural law:

1. The equality of all men is so evident that it is beyond question;

2. This self-evident universal equality is the basis upon which all men have a duty of love amongst one-another. It is in the discharge of this duty that we have to each other that the maximum expressions of justice and charity shall be derived.

3. Under natural law, man, while having liberty, does not have license to destroy others or himself.

4. All men are the "workmanship" of an omnipotent creator. This is the origin of natural law under which man has the right to his own liberty, as well as obligations to not interfere or injure the enjoyment of these rights by others and further still owes a duty to preserve the right to liberty of others.

The purpose of this text is to spark reform in the information age of the 21st Century. The 21st Century is a world that is heavily impacted by the development of the United States, in particular its development of that of a growing world power from the time of its Civil War to the present. The United States is a nation whose existence is based upon the philosophical tenets of Locke, with particular emphasis upon his *Two Treatises on Government.* To reinforce the validity of this observation, the following tables comparatively show excerpts from the *Declaration of Independence and The United States Constitution* in column format, compared directly to the text of *Two Treatises:*

Declaration of Independence	Two Treatises on Government
"…All men are created equal, that they are endowed by their Creator with certain unalienable Rights, that among these are Life, Liberty and the pursuit of Happiness"	"…A state also of equality wherein all the power and jurisdiction is reciprocal, no having more than another"
Prudence, indeed, will dictate that Governments long established should not be changed for light and transient causes; and accordingly all experience hath shewn, that mankind are more disposed to suffer, while evils are sufferable, than to right themselves by abolishing the	People are not so easily got out of their old forms, as some are apt to suggest. They are hardly to be prevailed with to amend the acknowledged faults in the frame they have been accustomed to. And if there be any original defects, or adventitious ones introduced by time, or corruption; it is not

forms to which they are accustomed an easy thing to get them changed, even when all the world sees there is an opportunity for it. This slowness and aversion in the people to quit their old constitutions, has, in the many revolutions which have been seen in this kingdom, in this and former ages, still kept us to, or, after some interval of fruitless attempts, still brought us back again to our old legislative of king, lords and commons: and whatever provocations have made the crown be taken from some of our princes heads, they never carried the people so far as to place it in another line.

But when a long train of abuses and usurpations, pursuing invariably the same Object evinces a design to reduce them under absolute Despotism, it is their right, it is their duty, to throw off such Government, and to provide new Guards for their future security

....But if a long train of abuses, prevarications and artifices, all tending the same way, make the design visible to the people, and they cannot but feel what they lie under, and see whither they are going; it is not to be wondered, that they should then rouze themselves, and endeavor to put the rule into such hands which may secure to them the ends for which government was at first erected; and without which, ancient names, and specious forms, are so far from being better, that they are much worse, than the state of nature, or pure anarchy; the inconveniencies being all as

	great and as near, but the remedy farther off and more difficult.

The United States Constitution	*Two Treatises on Government*
"All legislative Powers herein granted shall be vested in a Congress of the United States, which shall consist of a Senate and House of Representatives."	"...As it may be too great a temptation to human frailty, apt to grasp at power, for the same persons, who have the power of making laws, to have also in their hands the power to execute them."
"The executive Power shall be vested in a President of the United States of America."	"...which has the right to direct how the force of the commonwealth should be
"The judicial Power of the United States, shall be vested in one supreme Court, and in such inferior Courts as the	employed," the executive power to pursue the "perpetual execution" of established law, and the federative power

Congress may from time to time ordain and establish."	which contains the power of war and peace, leagues and alliances, with all persons and communities without the commonwealth."

Locke's theories of equality and justice align with the underlying truth of interconnectivity. His recommendation for a form of Government aligns with the recognition of equality amongst all people, which harmonizes with the truth of the interconnectivity of all things. The increase of information distribution via the printed word must be considered a major influence on the development of Locke's thinking as well the ability to widely distribute his works. Thereby magnifying its effects on the Governmental reforms of the 17th and 18th Centuries.

D. English and American Revolution

    i.   <u>17th Century England-</u> *The English Civil War(s) (1642 – 1651) and The Glorious Revolution (1688)*: This era in English history is largely concerned with the movement away from the Divine Right of Kings and the beginning of a shift in power from the Monarch to Parliament. Through his association with Anthony Ashley Cooper Lord Shatesbury, Locke lived in exile in the Netherlands following the Restoration of the Monarchy under Charles II in 1660, where Locke became part of the inner circle of William and Mary; so much so that Locke sailed from his exile in The Netherlands back to London aboard the same ship which carried then Princess Mary. To explore the connection between Locke and *The Glorious Revolution,* consider the following excerpt from *Locke, Lokean Ideals and the Glorious Revolution (*Schwoerer n.d.):

> *"In theory Locke held that government is dis-solved when either the legislative or the*

executive violates its trust, a concept central to his response to the Revolution. He explained in the Second Treatise that men in a state of nature create a community by entering into a contract, but that the community entrusts power to a government in a fiduciary relationship rather than a contractual one. This meant that if the governor violated his trust, the government was dissolved and the people had the right to resist. When a dissolution occurred power reverted to the people.

"In the preface to his Two Treatises he expressed the hope that his work would "make good" King William's title "in the consent of the people" and would justify "to the world the people of England, whose love of their just and natural rights, with

their resolution to preserve them, saved the

nation,"

It seems reasonable to assert that Locke's work was more influential on the transition following *The Glorious Revolution* then it was in the conflict itself. Reforms beginning in the reign of William and Mary manifest as the continuing notion of a Government through the consent of the people for the purpose of securing the enjoyment of their Natural Rights, specifically the adoption of The English Bill of Rights, which among other things, affected the transition to a Constitutional rather than Absolute Monarchy.

ii.   American Revolution and Natural Law – It seems most effective and authoritative, in the interest of understanding the connection between Natural Law and The American Revolution to provide an analysis of the original text of *The Declaration of Independence*:

IN CONGRESS, July 4, 1776.

The unanimous Declaration of the thirteen united States of America,

When in the Course of human events, it becomes necessary for one people to dissolve the political bands which have connected them with another, and to assume among the powers of the earth, the separate and equal station to which the Laws of Nature and of Nature's God entitle them, a decent respect to the opinions of mankind requires that they should declare the causes which impel them to the separation.

We hold these truths to be self-evident, that all men are created equal, that they are endowed by their Creator with certain unalienable Rights, that among these are Life, Liberty and the pursuit of Happiness.--That to secure these rights, Governments are instituted among Men, deriving their just powers from the consent of the governed, --That whenever any Form of Government becomes destructive of these ends, it is the Right of the People to alter or to abolish it, and to institute new

Government, laying its foundation on such principles and organizing its powers in such form, as to them shall seem most likely to effect their Safety and Happiness. Prudence, indeed, will dictate that Governments long established should not be changed for light and transient causes; and accordingly all experience hath shewn, that mankind are more disposed to suffer, while evils are sufferable, than to right themselves by abolishing the forms to which they are accustomed. But when a long train of abuses and usurpations, pursuing invariably the same Object evinces a design to reduce them under absolute Despotism, it is their right, it is their duty, to throw off such Government, and to provide new Guards for their future security.--Such has been the patient sufferance of these Colonies; and such is now the necessity which constrains them to alter their former Systems of Government. The history of the present King of Great Britain is a history of repeated injuries and usurpations, all having in direct object the establishment of an absolute Tyranny over these States. To prove this, let Facts be submitted to a candid world:

He has refused his Assent to Laws, the most wholesome and necessary for the public good.

He has forbidden his Governors to pass Laws of immediate and pressing importance, unless suspended in their operation till his Assent should be obtained; and when so suspended, he has utterly neglected to attend to them.

He has refused to pass other Laws for the accommodation of large districts of people, unless those people would relinquish the right of Representation in the Legislature, a right inestimable to them and formidable to tyrants only.

He has called together legislative bodies at places unusual, uncomfortable, and distant from the depository of their public Records, for the sole purpose of fatiguing them into compliance with his measures.

He has dissolved Representative Houses repeatedly, for opposing with manly firmness his invasions on the rights of the people.

He has refused for a long time, after such dissolutions, to cause others to be elected; whereby the Legislative powers, incapable of

Annihilation, have returned to the People at large for their exercise; the State remaining in the mean time exposed to all the dangers of invasion from without, and convulsions within.

He has endeavoured to prevent the population of these States; for that purpose obstructing the Laws for Naturalization of Foreigners; refusing to pass others to encourage their migrations hither, and raising the conditions of new Appropriations of Lands.

He has obstructed the Administration of Justice, by refusing his Assent to Laws for establishing Judiciary powers.

He has made Judges dependent on his Will alone, for the tenure of their offices, and the amount and payment of their salaries.

He has erected a multitude of New Offices, and sent hither swarms of Officers to harass our people, and eat out their substance.

He has kept among us, in times of peace, Standing Armies without the Consent of our legislatures.

He has affected to render the Military independent of and superior to the Civil power.

He has combined with others to subject us to a jurisdiction foreign to our constitution, and unacknowledged by our laws; giving his Assent to their Acts of pretended Legislation:

For Quartering large bodies of armed troops among us:

For protecting them, by a mock Trial, from punishment for any Murders which they should commit on the Inhabitants of these States:

For cutting off our Trade with all parts of the world:

For imposing Taxes on us without our Consent:

For depriving us in many cases, of the benefits of Trial by Jury:

For transporting us beyond Seas to be tried for pretended offences

For abolishing the free System of English Laws in a neighbouring Province, establishing therein an Arbitrary government, and enlarging its Boundaries so as to render it at once an example and fit instrument for introducing the same absolute rule into these Colonies:

For taking away our Charters, abolishing our most valuable Laws, and altering fundamentally the Forms of our Governments:

For suspending our own Legislatures, and declaring themselves invested with power to legislate for us in all cases whatsoever.

He has abdicated Government here, by declaring us out of his Protection and waging War against us.

He has plundered our seas, ravaged our Coasts, burnt our towns, and destroyed the lives of our people.

He is at this time transporting large Armies of foreign Mercenaries to compleat the works of death, desolation and tyranny, already begun with circumstances of Cruelty & perfidy scarcely paralleled in the most barbarous ages, and totally unworthy the Head of a civilized nation.

He has constrained our fellow Citizens taken Captive on the high Seas to bear Arms against their Country, to become the executioners of their friends and Brethren, or to fall themselves by their   Hands.

He has excited domestic insurrections amongst us, and has endeavoured to bring on the inhabitants of our frontiers, the merciless Indian Savages, whose known rule of warfare, is an undistinguished destruction of all ages, sexes and conditions.

In every stage of these Oppressions We have petitioned for Redress in the most humble terms: Our repeated Petitions have been answered only by repeated injury. A Prince whose character is thus marked by every act which may define a Tyrant, is unfit to be the ruler of a free people.

Nor have We been wanting in attentions to our British brethren. We have warned them from time to time of attempts by their legislature to extend an unwarrantable jurisdiction over us. We have reminded them of the circumstances of our emigration and settlement here. We have appealed to their native justice and magnanimity, and we have conjured them by the ties of our common kindred to disavow these usurpations, which, would inevitably interrupt our connections and correspondence. They too have been deaf to the voice of justice and of consanguinity. We must, therefore, acquiesce in the necessity, which denounces our Separation, and hold them, as we hold the rest of mankind, Enemies in War, in Peace Friends.

We, therefore, the Representatives of the united States of America, in General Congress, Assembled, appealing to the Supreme Judge of the world for the rectitude of our intentions, do, in the Name, and by Authority of the good People of these Colonies, solemnly publish and declare, That these United Colonies are, and of Right ought to be Free and Independent States; that they are Absolved from all Allegiance to the British Crown, and that all political connection between them and the State of Great Britain, is and ought to be totally dissolved; and that as Free and Independent States, they have full Power to levy War, conclude Peace, contract Alliances, establish Commerce, and to do all other Acts and Things which Independent States may of right do. And for the *support of this Declaration, with a firm reliance on the protection*

of divine Providence, we mutually pledge to each other our Lives,

our Fortunes and our sacred Honor.

Consider these following excerpts which reinforce that Natural
Law is the philosophical underpinning and the basic social
contract of *The United States of America:*

1. ...assume among the powers of the earth, the separate and equal

station to which the Laws of Nature and of Nature's God entitle

them

2. ... We hold these truths to be self-evident, that all men are

created equal, that they are endowed by their Creator with certain

unalienable Rights, that among these are Life, Liberty and the

pursuit of Happiness.--That to secure these rights, Governments

are instituted among Men, deriving their just powers from the

consent of the governed, --That whenever any Form of

Government becomes destructive of these ends, it is the Right of

the People to alter or to abolish it, and to institute new

Government, laying its foundation on such principles and

organizing its powers in such form, as to them shall seem most

likely to effect their Safety and Happiness. Prudence, indeed, will dictate that Governments long established should not be changed for light and transient causes; and accordingly all experience hath shewn, that mankind are more disposed to suffer, while evils are sufferable, than to right themselves by abolishing the forms to which they are accustomed. But when a long train of abuses and usurpations, pursuing invariably the same Object evinces a design to reduce them under absolute Despotism, it is their right, it is their duty, to throw off such Government, and to provide new Guards for their future security.

3.... We, therefore, the Representatives of the united States of America, in General Congress, Assembled, appealing to the Supreme Judge of the world for the rectitude of our intentions

4. And for the support of this Declaration, with a firm reliance on the protection of divine Providence, we mutually pledge to each other our Lives, our Fortunes and our sacred Honor.

The Declaration of Independence clearly sets forth that the people of the to-be-formed United States invoked *Natural Law*. Being that Natural Law is built on the Self-Evident Truth that all men have equal station to one another, and as governments are instituted among men to preserve and protect the right to equally enjoy the rights arising from this natural and equal station, it is the right and duty of men to dissolve any form of government which becomes corrupt and adverse to the equal enjoyment of natural rights amongst its people. It is also unequivocal, that a *Supreme Judge of the World and Divine Providence* is the source and origin of *Natural Law*. While it is essential and clear that in the United States, that its government is founded upon a recognition of the essential and truthful nature of an omnipotent Supreme Judge who moves man's development, especially his development of social, governmental and economic system, manifest as his Divine Providence. This is not in any way inconsistent with the separation of Church and State. While it is contrary to Natural Law that a Governmental System mandate and individual's process of salvation and individual means of spiritual discovery, Natural Law exists only as an extension of Nature which is a manifestation of an omnipotent, omnipresent Supreme Judge, God or a Singularity.

E.   Adam Smith's Philosophy and Economic Theories

The central purpose of this work is to demonstrate that the true nature of the universe is that of a singular essence through which all is connected, masked in paradox and deception. From this starting point, man has constructed governmental, social and economic systems over the millennia as a function of his false belief in the deception of scarcity. During the Enlightenment, fueled by the aid to reasoning ability provided by the printed word, man began to pierce through to truth. In particular the precepts of *Natural Law* as described in the works of John Locke posit a fundamental equality amongst men. This accelerated the pace of reform. Since the 17th century, governmental forms took root based upon these philosophical tenants. As was previously mentioned, governmental systems built upon *Natural Law* with economic systems being still foundationally built upon the deceptive nature of resource scarcity have made little impact upon the emergence of genuine equality and universal justice.

The economic theories of Smith as set forth in *Wealth of Nations* have laid the foundation of our modern world far more than have

Locke's theories on Natural Law. To clearly observe the belief system of Smith, excerpts of key ideas from both of his seminal works: *Wealth of Nations* and *Theory on Moral Sentiments* are presented

Theory on Moral Sentiment:

"The administration of the great system of the universe, however, the care of the universal happiness of all rational and sensible beings, is the business of God and not of man. To man is allotted a much humbler department, but one much more suitable to the weakness of his powers, and to the narrowness of his comprehension; the care of his own happiness, of that of his family, his friends, his country."

"But every part of nature, when attentively surveyed, equally demonstrates the providential care of its Author, and we may admire the wisdom and goodness of God even in the weakness and folly of man."

The notions of Smith disclosed herein are more *Machiavellian* in their nature than they are *Lockean*. It may be useful yet again the recall the following excerpt from Machiavelli's *The Prince:*

"For of men it may generally be affirmed, that they are thankless, fickle, false, studious to avoid danger, greedy of gain, devoted to you while you are able to confer benefits upon them".

As we have seen, the notions of Locke on Natural law are clearly evident and congruent with the notions expressed in The Declaration of Independence, whereby equality and justice and noble self-sacrifice are virtues of man. Machiavelli and Smith, on the other hand, hold that the dark elements of man's nature, his folly, weakness, ingratitude, self-centered and deceptive nature, are those upon which systems and governance must consider to be sustainable and effective. While it is abundantly clear that as a function of the universal paradox or stated alternatively satanic deception, man falsely posited temporal scarcity (death), which gives rise to economic scarcity as a function thereof. He then constructed his social and economic systems based upon this false premise. It follows therefore that his behaviors would align with this false premise. The observations by Machiavelli and Smith of man's self-centered behavior has copious evidence to support its validity. Regardless, this behavior is built upon a false premise of scarcity that can and must be adjusted if we ever hope to develop

176

a construct in which harmony, peace, equality and justice emerge, and poverty, oppression and war vanish.

Connecting Smith's philosophy to his economic theory, please consider this excerpt from *Wealth of Nations:*

> *Wealth, as Mr. Hobbes says, is power. But the person who either acquires, or succeeds to a great fortune, does not necessarily acquire or succeed to any political power, either civil or military. His fortune may, perhaps, afford him the means of acquiring both, but the mere possession of that fortune does not necessarily convey to him either. The power which that possession immediately and directly conveys to him, is the power of purchasing; a certain command over all the labour, or over all the produce of labour which is then in the market. His fortune is greater or less, precisely in proportion to the extent of this power; or to the quantity either of other men's labour, or, what is the same thing, of the produce of other men's labour, which it enables him to purchase or command. The exchangeable value of every thing must always be precisely equal to the extent of this power which it conveys to its owner"*

It again is *Self-Evident*, that the underlying philosophy of Smith is oriented on the broken, disconnected, sinful and non-atoned nature of men. It follows then, to quell the angst of the powerlessness that arises from man's tragic flaws and shortcomings that he would seek out a haven from these weaknesses. "Wealth is power", as Smith invokes Thomas Hobbes. It is the power to command the labor of others. It is again *Self-Evident* that this imagery is incongruent with universal oneness and harmony, while it is entirely congruent with the notion of self-preservation motivated by the fear which arises from the sinful or fallen, or non-atoned, disconnected and therefore limited perspective on truth arising from *Original Sin* or if you prefer *Satanic Deception or Paradox*. To reinforce yet again consider the following words of Satan from Milton's *Paradise Lost:*

"Better to reign in hell than to serve in Heaven"

The parallels between this satanic observation, and the notions of the power assumed by man through wealth accumulation are again, *Self-evident.* Lastly please consider 1 Timothy 6:10:

"For the love of money is the root of many evils"

To summarize, the theories of Adam Smith undergird our econo0mic system. They shape life in the 21st century far more directly than does the Lockean theory of Natural Law which is the foundational principal that our society is ostensibly ordered upon. Further, the theories of Adam Smith as has been shown here are based upon philosophical underpinning of sinful, fallen or non-atoned man. It follows therefore that Smith's theories are driven upon the sinful notion of temporal scarcity, which as has been previously demonstrated here, is the root of economic scarcity. This dynamic is inherently sinful and shall therefore never produce a social system in which harmony and justice emerges. It will continue in perpetuity, to produce disharmony, chaos, poverty and war.

F. State sanctioned injustice: Imperialism, Slavery and Social
    Darwinism

The resilience of the paradoxical or satanic force is quite formidable. As man began to see through to the foundational truth of interconnectivity, these breakthroughs seemed to have been followed by a new resolve of darkness. Reforms in England moving power away from the monarchy and into the hands of the people's representatives upon the theory of the equality of all men, was followed by the economic injustices and exploitation of Imperialism. Jefferson himself who so powerfully refined and applied Lockean Ideals for the New World owned slaves himself. The original text of the Constitution while silent on the issue of slavery set forth the "Three-fifths rule" for the purpose of determining the impact to congressional representation that slave populations warranted. This Constitutional language remained until 1866. Just after the civil war this language was replaced through the ratification of the 14th Amendment.

It is *Self-evident* that imperialism and slavery are fundamentally inconsistent with the precepts of *Natural Law*. How then, in the wake of the Revolutionary era in which the righteous basis of the equality of man and universal justice, can man backslide into the darkness of self-centered economic conduct?

Clearly the drive in man to find universal truth, which led to the recognition of *Natural Law* as the righteous basis for a harmonious and peaceful society, is in counterbalance with man's Machiavellian drives. The spell of the universal paradox which plagues the mind of man is formidable, wily and cunning. Man's strongly but falsely held belief in the satanic deception of separation is deep, it has a substantial moment of inertia. Nonetheless, on the heels of Locke, Adam Smith's theories lay the philosophical basis for the righteousness of the sinful and self-centered thoughts which justify inhumanities in the name of wealth accumulation. Unfortunately Smith's theory is built upon deception. Economic scarcity is invalid as a precept as it is a function of existential and temporal scarcity, which as has been previously demonstrated herein is a false precept.

To further provide justification, albeit false justification for the oppressions and exploitations of both slavery and imperialism, 19th century Social Darwinists endeavored to underwrite the propriety of oppression based upon the notion of a social and economic survival of the fittest.

Consider the following from Herbert Spencer's *Social Statistics:*

> *"The forces which are working out the great scheme of perfect happiness, taking no account of incidental suffering, exterminate such sections of mankind as stand in their way, with the same sternness that they exterminate beasts of prey and herds of useless ruminants."*

> *"This universal law of physical modification, is the law of mental modification also. The multitudinous differences of capacity and disposition that have in course of time grown up between the Indian, African, Mongolian and Caucasian races, and between the various subdivisions of them, must all be ascribed to the acquirement in each case of fitness for surrounding circumstances. Those strong contrasts between the characters of nations and of times awhile since exemplified admit of no other conceivable explanation. Why all this divergence from the one common original type? If adaptation of constitution to conditions is not the cause, what is the cause?"*

"The development of the higher creation is a progress towards a form of being capable of a happiness undiminished by these drawbacks. It is in the human race that the consummation is to be accomplished. Civilization is the last stage of its accomplishment. And the ideal man is the man in whom all the conditions of that accomplishment are fulfilled. Meanwhile the well-being of existing humanity, and the unfolding of it into this ultimate perfection, are both secured by that same beneficent, though severe discipline, to which the animate creation at large is subject: a discipline which is pitiless in the working out of good: a felicity-pursuing law which never swerves for the avoidance of partial and temporary suffering. The poverty of the incapable, the distresses that come upon the imprudent, the starvation of the idle, and those shoulderings aside of the weak by the strong, which leave so many "in shallows and in miseries," are the decrees of a large, far-seeing benevolence."

Clearly, Herbert Spenser's philosophy which rationalizes that the plight of the impoverished, whereby they are left *"in shallows and in misery"* is a decree of *"Far Seeing Benevolence"*, is incongruent with the precepts of Natural Law and are inconsistent with the interconnectivity of all things. It is clearly congruent with the paradoxical and satanic deception of temporal and economic scarcity, and aligns the philosophies of Machiavelli and the economic theory of Smith.

G. Conclusion

As we have demonstrated here the Printing Press acted as an incubator for the intellectual expansions of the Protestant Reformation, the Scientific Revolution and the Enlightenment. Man is driven to discover truth. His reach for universal truth is expanded through technological innovations which accelerate the pace at which new ideas can be circulated, analyzed, debated and improved upon.

The birth of the notion of universal equality and justice as the only righteous basis for governmental systems is a function of these developments. Governmental forms however are the beginning rather that the end of the process. To rationalize the economic structures that man has grown accustomed to especially those that seem to give rise to the maximum expression of a man, that being massive accumulated wealth, the application of Social Darwinistic philosophical theories sought to underwrite the righteousness of ruthless and self-centered economic practices and systems. Those civilizations and individuals that are not optimally driven to wealth accumulation by all means possible become the means of wealth consolidation by those who are. The application of

Darwin's theories to human socioeconomic behavior legitimizes and makes righteous the most illegitimate and unrighteous of oppressive, deceptive and evil behavior in the name of maximizing wealth accumulation. And the beat goes on.

References:

Steinberg, S., & Trevitt, J. (1996). *Five hundred years of printing* (New ed.). London: British Library

Schwoerer, L. (n.d.). Locke, Lockean Ideas, and the Glorious Revolution. *Journal of the History of Ideas,* 531-531.

IX. The American Centuries

A. Introduction

The purpose of this chapter is to examine the impact that the philosophies of the Social Darwinists, Machiavelli and Adam Smith have asserted on the rise of American's economic and military power since the Civil War. In 21st century America, fueled by the economic theories of Adam Smith and the philosophies of the Machiavelli and the Social Darwinists, a foundational corruption of the money supply has occurred. Under the *United States Constitution* it is the obligation of the Congress to investigate and punish this type of crime. It is the only crime mentioned directly in the Constitution, that being the crime of *Counterfeiting*. It is also the only crime capable of destroying the Republic and it nearly has. The modern practices of securitization and speculative financial instrument trading has given rise to a process through which control of the resources of this nation have become consolidated in the hands of the few. This process has in turn given rise to discontinuities in the production of essential services such as housing, health-care, education, infrastructure and provisions for old age.

The uninvestigated systemic and institutional crime of *Counterfeiting* is not yet on the American public's radar screen. It is concealed in the most diabolical of places, right under our noses. The process of campaign finance, specifically for members of the United States Congress as their duty includes the regulation of the currency and the investigation and punishment of Counterfeiting offenses, whereby they raise money to seek elected office from the very elements of society waging this economic war upon the Republic and the people of the United States, ensures this affront to natural law which has given rise to massive wealth consolidation at the direct expense of the basic needs of the American People will continue uninvestigated, unpunished and unadjusted. This paradigm is justified under the very same theories of Adam Smith and the Social Darwinists that rationalized the injustices of Imperialism and Slavery. The existing economic paradigm denies large segments of the American people their fundamental Natural rights. It is an affront to Natural Law and a violation of the Constitution of the United States. Those who drive and defend this paradigm are domestic enemies of the state. It is the duty of this generation to identify these crimes, make righteous adjustments to correct their effects upon the

American people and *"Provide new guards for our future security."*

This chapter shall explore the evolution of American society and its economic constructs since the Civil War. It shall demonstrate that the paradoxical and satanic has effectively blinded this nation against the underlying truth of interconnectivity and oneness that it was ostensibly founded upon, the notion that all men were created equal. The embodiment of the Robber Barron generation as the ideal model of American manhood and success hangs as a dark shadow on the soul of this nation, driving it perpetually to chaos and disharmony which shall continue to be the results of a society whose economic system is based upon the deception of scarcity. Once again, it is the duty of this generation of Americans to bring clarity and understanding to the darkness and unsustainability of its current economic paradigm and install new economic systems founded upon the ideals of justice and equality.

B. American Slavery and its legacy

While it presents as *Self-Evident* that the philosophical justification for slavery arises from the blindness to interconnected truth which lays at the root of the American Republic, it nonetheless may prove useful reinforcement to consider the observations of those who sought to provide a moral justification for slavery. Consider the following excerpt from an address delivered by Henry Thornwell to the General Assembly of the Presbyterian Church on May 16, 1861. Thornwell was a Presbyterian Minister who became an outspoken advocate for the Confederacy and the institution of slavery (Teaching American History Website):

> ...*Indeed, the first organization of the church as a visible society, separate and distinct from the unbelieving world, was inaugurated in the family of a slaveholder [Abraham]. Among the very first persons to whom the seal of circumcision was affixed were the slaves of the father of the faithful, some born in his house and others bought with his money. Slavery again reappears under the Law. God sanctions it in the first table of the Decalogue, and Moses treats it as an institution to be regulated, not abolished;*

legitimated and not condemned. We come down to the age of the New Testament, and we find it again in the churches founded by the apostles under the plenary inspiration of the Holy Ghost. These facts are utterly amazing, if slavery is the enormous sin which its enemies represent it to be. It will not do to say that the Scriptures have treated it only in a general, incidental way, without any clear implication as to its moral character. Moses surely made it the subject of express and positive legislation, and the apostles are equally explicit in inculcating the duties which spring from both sides of the relation. They treat slaves as bound to obey and inculcate obedience as an office of religion a thing wholly self-contradictory if the authority exercised over them were unlawful and iniquitous.

...As to the endless declamation about human rights, we have only to say that human rights are not a fixed but fluctuating quantity. Their sum is not the same in any two nations on the globe. The rights of Englishmen are one thing, the rights of Frenchmen, another. There is a minimum without which a man cannot be responsible;

there is a maximum which expresses the highest degree of

civilization and of Christian culture.

Thornwell proves useful as he clearly states *"....as to the endless declamation about human rights, we have only to say that human rights are not a fixed but fluctuating quantity. Their sum is not the same in any two nations on the globe. The rights of the Englishmen are one thing, the rights of Frenchman another."* Simple and to the point, the justification for slavery requires a moral basis upon which one can neatly and eloquently dispose of the notions of *Natural Rights,* equality and justice.

The study of the righteousness of racial inequality and economic exclusion has been a pestilence upon the African American community and by extension the American people in general, its effects continue 150 years after the Civil War and the final abolition of slavery.

The plight of African Americans in contemporary America presents a very useful visual to examine the effects of the universal paradox upon American society and how we remain practically blind to the truth of interconnectivity. The difference in skin color between whites and blacks while seemingly of no practical relevance, may lay very near to the root of man's paradoxically or if you prefer satanically induced blindness to universal interconnectivity. It is useful once again to describe the universal paradox (from section III of this text):

1.) All is one;

2.) Existence as a series of experiences or interactions requires more than one element;

3.) There is not more than one element;

4.) The foregoing are mutually exclusive, yet both are true;

5.) It follows therefore that the existence of the universe balances on Paradox

As was previously demonstrated herein, through an analysis of quantum experimentation and scriptural analysis the fundamental nature of the universe is that of a singular cohesive field which resides in quantum superposition, non-locally, or stated alternatively outside the four dimensions of space-time which collapses into space-time as a function of observation. At the moment of this collapse into space-time these elemental particles remain interconnected. This connection resides outside the boundaries of space-time. All things are constructed of these elemental particles. It follows therefore that everything is quantumly entangled thusly. To reiterate, the universe's true nature is that of interconnected cohesive singularity, wrapped in paradoxical or satanic deception to create the illusion of separation or differentiation to facilitate the interactions that are required to exist. Our minds are designed to gravitate to differences thusly. Through this observation we falsely perceive separation and differentiation. The first result of seeing the universe in this manner is the observation that the time for my fully separated essence to exist is scarce. I dwell in the valley of the shadow of death.

To improve the quality of my limited existence over inaccurately perceived finite time, my consciousness seeks out to deaden the chaos of this disharmony by expanding time. I errantly believe that I may expand time in human society through the acquisition and accumulation of wealth. Through accumulated wealth I assert power to require the services of others which are a function of their time being sequestered to my service. In order to justify the process which maximizes my efficiency in harvesting the time of others, the philosophies of the Social Darwinists are of great value. It forms the basis upon which the atrocities of slavery and imperialism were rationalized and justified.

The difference in skin color between white and black Americans acts as an amplifier of the deception of separation and differentiation. Coupled with the continuing economic legacy of slavery, the blindness of Americans to recognize that the presence of the Satanic or Paradoxical as an amplifying factor in the disharmony between white and black America, contributes to its perpetuation as it is a strong echo of the deception of differentiation.

Consider the following observations of Glenn Loury on the continuing effects that the injustice of slavery asserts on contemporary African American society and by extension upon American society in general (Loury 1995):

> *"As anyone even vaguely aware of the social conditions in contemporary America knows, we still face a "problem of the color line." The dream that race might someday become an insignificant category in our civic life now*

seems naively utopian. In cities across the country, and in rural areas of the Old South, the situation of the black underclass and, increasingly, of the black lower working classes is bad and getting worse. No well-informed person denies this, though there is debate over what can and should be done about it. Nor do serious people deny that the crime, drug addiction, family breakdown, unemployment, poor school performance, welfare dependency, and general decay in these communities constitute a blight on our society virtually unrivaled in scale and severity by anything to be found elsewhere in the industrial West."

Summary – The theories of the Social Darwinists provided moral justification for both slavery and the injustices perpetrated upon African Americans since the end of slavery. The stain of racial injustice that hangs on America provides a very clear visual of the operations of the paradoxical and satanic in contemporary America. Blinded to truth, man seeks out and rationalizes differentiation, it is in this rationalized differentiation that we have found the continuing justification to practically speaking, deny the enjoyment of fundamental Natural Rights, equality and justice. It is the law of the land, but it is not yet the American Reality as the American Reality is a function of the economic theories of Adam Smith and the philosophical theories of the Machiavelli and the Social Darwinists which are affronts to Natural Law, the United States Constitution and the dignity of the American people and from which the cycle of war, poverty and crime shall never cease.

C. Civil War

The purpose of this text is to demonstrate that the interconnected nature of the universe is its true and natural state. The results of quantum experimentation as well as an analysis of scripture clearly and unequivocally provide us a means to see this truth, or stated alternatively we have discovered the path back to gaining our sustenance from the Tree of Life. The nature of the universe is that of a singular interconnected field wrapped in paradox or satanic deception in order to create the false perception that individual elements of the universe are genuinely separated from one another. As has been stated previously this is essential to facilitate existence which is a series of experiences over time. To have experiences requires more than one element and as was demonstrated previously there is not more than one element, hence the need for a force which exists to create deception.

The nature of the singularity in paradox is evident in the affairs of man. On the heels of the enlightenment the observations of Locke on Natural Law, the natural state of equality and justice amongst all men harmonizes with the interconnected nature of reality, as that reality's nature is proven true through quantum experimentation as well as an analysis of scripture. The active effects of the satanic or paradoxical membrane are a resilient factor in the affairs of man. The observations on Natural Law and its appropriate place as the foundation of social systems began to take root in the proliferation of constitutional forms of government beginning in the 17th and 18th centuries. Notwithstanding this breakthrough, in seeing the genuine truth of oneness the mind of man remains susceptible to the delusion of separation and disconnection. As has been discussed here, this mindset is sinful in the most genuine sense of this term, that being one of inaccuracy. To remind the reader once again:

"The wages of sin is Death"

Romans 6:23

Being continually possessed of this faulty or sinful mindset, man falsely perceives his separation from the balance of the universe and from that perspective, he dwells all the days of his life under the specter of death. Death is a function of finite time, the logical response of men who perceive the limitation of time is to seek to acquire claims upon the time of other men. The accumulation of monetized wealth is precisely just that.

Consider once again the words of Satan from Milton's *Paradise Lost:*

"Better to reign in Hell than serve in Heaven"

As a nation, the United States has shaped life in the 21st century perhaps as much as any nation has ever effected life upon the earth. As such, the practices which have shaped life in 21st century America warrant careful reflection. The United States is a nation that is ostensibly founded upon the notions of Natural Law, Equality and Justice. These principal clearly harmonize with the true construct of the universe that of an interconnected singular field wrapped in paradox. Regardless of the laws and governmental forms of the United States, its economic construct violates the tenants of Natural Law. Its economic practices align with the philosophies of the Social Darwinists, Adam Smith and Machiavelli. It follows therefore that the economic system of the United States, and by extension that of the world in the 21st century is one of systematic disharmony. The egregious disparity in wealth distribution is the basis upon which poverty, war and crime are perpetuated.

There is perhaps no better illustrative, which makes clear the distinction between the Natural Law based society envisioned in the Declaration of Independence and the United States Constitution, and the economic and social realities of the United States than does the institution of slavery.

In this section we shall evaluate two of the most impactful speeches during the time of the Civil War. In what has become known as the *"Cornerstone Speech"*. Alexander Stevens, Vice President of the Confederacy delivered a speech which clearly describes the Social Darwinistic philosophy which was the foundation of the Confederacy. In contrast, Abraham Lincoln's Second Inaugural Address clearly validates the righteousness of equality and natural law and that the enslavement of men is a scourge.

Alexander Steven's *Cornerstone Speech* was delivered on March 21, 1861. From December 1860 through the date of the speech the following seven states seceded from the Union: South Carolina, Mississippi, Florida, Alabama, Georgia, Louisiana and Texas. 22 days after this speech the Confederates fired upon Fort Sumter, initiating hostilities of the American Civil War. In his book, "*A new birth of freedom: Abraham Lincoln and the coming of the Civil War,*" Harry Jaffa, referring to the *Cornerstone Speech, states that*:

> """...*this remarkable address conveys, more than any other contemporary document, not only the soul of the Confederacy but also of the Jim Crow South that arose from the ashes of the Confederacy.*" *(Jaffa, 2000)*

The following is an excerpt of the text of this speech:

> ...*allow me to allude to one other though last, not least. The new constitution has put at rest, forever, all the agitating questions relating to our peculiar institution African slavery as it exists amongst us the proper status of the Negro in our form of civilization. This was the immediate cause of the late rupture and present revolution. Jefferson in his forecast, had anticipated this, as the "rock upon which the old Union would split." He was right. What was conjecture with him, is now a realized fact. But whether he fully comprehended the great truth upon which that rock stood and stands, may be doubted. The prevailing*

ideas entertained by him and most of the leading statesmen at the time of the formation of the old constitution, were that the enslavement of the African was in violation of the laws of nature; that it was wrong in principle, socially, morally, and politically. It was an evil they knew not well how to deal with, but the general opinion of the men of that day was that, somehow or other in the order of Providence, the institution would be evanescent and pass away. This idea, though not incorporated in the constitution, was the prevailing idea at that time. The constitution, it is true, secured every essential guarantee to the institution while it should last, and hence no argument can be justly urged against the constitutional guarantees thus secured, because of the common sentiment of the day. Those ideas, however, were fundamentally wrong. They rested upon the assumption of the equality of races. This was an error. It was a sandy foundation, and the government built upon it fell when the "storm came and the wind blew."

Our new government is founded upon exactly the opposite idea; its foundations are laid, its corner- stone rests, upon

*the great truth that the Negro is not equal to the white man;
that slavery subordination to the superior race is his
natural and normal condition. This, our new government,
is the first, in the history of the world, based upon this great
physical, philosophical, and moral truth. This truth has
been slow in the process of its development, like all other
truths in the various departments of science. It has been so
even amongst us. Many who hear me, perhaps, can
recollect well, that this truth was not generally admitted,
even within their day. The errors of the past generation
still clung to many as late as twenty years ago. Those at
the North, who still cling to these errors, with a zeal above
knowledge, we justly denominate fanatics. All fanaticism
springs from an aberration of the mind from a defect in
reasoning. It is a species of insanity. One of the most
striking characteristics of insanity, in many instances, is
forming correct conclusions from fancied or erroneous
premises; so with the anti-slavery fanatics. Their
conclusions are right if their premises were. They assume
that the Negro is equal, and hence conclude that he is
entitled to equal privileges and rights with the white man.*

If their premises were correct, their conclusions would be logical and just but their premise being wrong, their whole argument fails. I recollect once of having heard a gentleman from one of the northern States, of great power and ability, announce in the House of Representatives, with imposing effect, that we of the South would be compelled, ultimately, to yield upon this subject of slavery, that it was as impossible to war successfully against a principle in politics, as it was in physics or mechanics. That the principle would ultimately prevail. That we, in maintaining slavery as it exists with us, were warring against a principle, a principle founded in nature, the principle of the equality of men. The reply I made to him was, that upon his own grounds, we should, ultimately, succeed, and that he and his associates, in this crusade against our institutions, would ultimately fail. The truth announced, that it was as impossible to war successfully against a principle in politics as it was in physics and mechanics, I admitted; but told him that it was he, and those acting with him, who were warring against a principle. They were attempting to make things equal which the Creator had made unequal.

In the conflict thus far, success has been on our side, complete throughout the length and breadth of the Confederate States. It is upon this, as I have stated, our social fabric is firmly planted; and I cannot permit myself to doubt the ultimate success of a full recognition of this principle throughout the civilized and enlightened world.

As I have stated, the truth of this principle may be slow in development, as all truths are and ever have been, in the various branches of science. It was so with the principles announced by Galileo it was so with Adam Smith and his principles of political economy. It was so with Harvey, and his theory of the circulation of the blood. It is stated that not a single one of the medical profession, living at the time of the announcement of the truths made by him, admitted them. Now, they are universally acknowledged. May we not, therefore, look with confidence to the ultimate universal acknowledgment of the truths upon which our system rests? It is the first government ever instituted upon

207

the principles in strict conformity to nature, and the ordination of Providence, in furnishing the materials of human society. Many governments have been founded upon the principle of the subordination and serfdom of certain classes of the same race; such were and are in violation of the laws of nature. Our system commits no such violation of nature's laws. With us, all of the white race, however high or low, rich or poor, are equal in the eye of the law. Not so with the Negro. Subordination is his place. He, by nature, or by the curse against Canaan, is fitted for that condition which he occupies in our system. The architect, in the construction of buildings, lays the foundation with the proper material-the granite; then comes the brick or the marble. The substratum of our society is made of the material fitted by nature for it, and by experience we know that it is best, not only for the superior, but for the inferior race, that it should be so. It is, indeed, in conformity with the ordinance of the Creator. It is not for us to inquire into the wisdom of His ordinances, or to question them. For His own purposes, He has made one race to differ from another, as He has made "one star *to differ from another star in glory." The great objects of humanity are best attained when there is conformity to His laws and decrees, in the formation of governments as well as in all things else. Our confederacy is founded upon principles in strict conformity with these laws. This stone which was rejected by the first builders "is become the chief of the corner" the real "corner-stone" in our new edifice. I have been asked, what of the future? It has been apprehended by some that we would have arrayed against us the civilized world. I care not who or how many they may be against us, when we stand upon the eternal principles of truth, if we are true to ourselves and the principles for which we contend, we are obliged to, and must triumph.*

Thousands of people who begin to understand these truths are not yet completely out of the shell; they do not see them in their length and breadth. We hear much of the civilization and Christianization of the barbarous tribes of Africa. In my judgment, those ends will never be attained, but by first teaching them the lesson taught to Adam, that "in the sweat of his brow he should eat his bread," and

teaching them to work, and feed, and clothe themselves.

Consider the following themes from *Cornerstone:*

1. The new constitution [Confederate Constitution] has put at rest, forever, all the agitating questions relating to our peculiar institution African slavery as it exists amongst us the proper status of the Negro in our form of civilization.

2. Jefferson in his forecast, had anticipated this, as the "rock upon which the old Union would split." He was right. What was conjecture with him, is now a realized fact. But whether he fully comprehended the great truth upon which that rock stood and stands, may be doubted. The prevailing ideas entertained by him and most of the leading statesmen at the time of the formation of the old constitution, were that the enslavement of the African was in violation of the laws of nature; that it was wrong in principle, socially, morally, and politically. It was an evil they knew not well how to deal with, but the general opinion of the men of that day was that, somehow or other in the order of Providence,

the institution would be evanescent and pass away. This idea, though not incorporated in the constitution, was the prevailing idea at that time. The constitution, it is true, secured every essential guarantee to the institution while it should last, and hence no argument can be justly urged against the constitutional guarantees thus secured, because of the common sentiment of the day. Those ideas, however, were fundamentally wrong. They rested upon the assumption of the equality of races. This was an error.

3. With us, all of the white race, however high or low, rich or poor, are equal in the eye of the law. Not so with the Negro. Subordination is his place. He, by nature, or by the curse against Canaan, is fitted for that condition which he occupies in our system.

4. It is, indeed, in conformity with the ordinance of the Creator. It is not for us to inquire into the wisdom of His ordinances, or to question them. For His own purposes, He has made one race to differ from another,

5. I care not who or how many they may be against us, when we stand upon the eternal principles of truth, if we are true to ourselves and the principles for which we contend, we are obliged to, and must triumph.

Steven's speech is an exceedingly valuable study. His logic and reasoning are exceptional if not flawless. However, as he starts his analysis upon a foundation of a lie, the inequality between races, he achieves only a successful defense of a falsehood and in this case a falsehood of the most diabolical and evil of natures. Not only does he eloquently observe inequality amongst the races, he goes further to suggest that Natural Law is indeed in error, insofar as it includes all races of men. To amplify the resilience and slipperiness of satanic deception, Mr. Steven invokes scripture and the Creator and Divine Providence as the true and righteous source of racial inferiority and that it not only is Divinely Ordained, that negros' proper role is that of property, eternally subjugated as unequals, not warranting any rights whatever, but further still, that the attempt to assert and defend equality between the races is the affront to Natural Law, the will of the Creator and of Divine Providence.

It is quite clear that after deep and thoughtful reflection, that Mr. Steven's philosophies, which as Jaffa observes is the "soul of the confederacy", are a function of the philosophies of the Machiavelli and the Social Darwinists and the economic theory of Adam Smith. They are clearly an affront to the ideals of Jefferson and Locke.

Lincoln's Second Inaugural Address:

In contrast to the *Cornerstone Speech,* which as Jaffa (2000) observes,"... [reflects] the soul of the Confederacy", consider Lincoln's *Second Inaugural Address:*

> *"At this second appearing, to take the oath of the Presidential office, there is less occasion for an extended address than there was at the first. Then a statement, somewhat in detail, of a course to be pursued, seemed fitting and proper. Now, at the expiration of four years, during which public declarations have been constantly called forth on every point and phase of the great contest*

213

which still absorbs the attention, and engrosses the energies of the nation, little that is new could be presented. The progress of our arms, upon which all else chiefly depends, is as well known to the public as to myself, and it is, I trust, reasonably satisfactory and encouraging to all. With high hope for the future, no prediction in regard to it is ventured.

On the occasion corresponding to this four years ago, all thoughts were anxiously directed to an impending civil war. All dreaded it—all sought to avert it. While the inaugural address was being delivered from this place, devoted altogether to saving the Union without war, insurgent agents were in the city seeking to destroy it without war—seeking to dissolve the Union, and divide effects by negotiation. Both parties deprecated war, but one of them would make war rather than let the nation survive; and the other would accept war rather than let it perish, and the war came. One-eighth of the whole population were colored slaves, not distributed generally over the Union, but localized in the southern part of it.

These slaves constituted a peculiar and powerful interest. All knew that this interest was somehow the cause of the war. To strengthen, perpetuate, and extend this interest was the object for which the insurgents would rend the Union, even by war; while the Government claimed no right to do more than to restrict the territorial enlargement of it.

Neither party expected for the war, the magnitude, or the duration, which it has already attained. Neither anticipated that the cause of the conflict might cease with, or even before, the conflict itself should cease. Each looked for an easier triumph, and a result less fundamental and astounding. Both read the same Bible, and pray to the same God; and each invokes His aid against the other. It may seem strange that any men should dare to ask a just God's assistance in wringing their bread from the sweat of other men's faces; but let us judge not, that we be not judged. The prayers of both could not be answered; that of neither has been answered fully. The Almighty has His own purposes. "Woe unto the world because of offenses; for it

215

must needs be that offenses come, but woe to that man by whom the offense cometh." If we shall suppose that American Slavery is one of those offenses which, in the providence of God, must needs come, but which, having continued through His appointed time, He now wills to remove, and that He gives to both North and South this terrible war, as the woe due to those by whom the offense came, shall we discern therein any departure from those divine attributes which the believers in a living God always ascribe to Him? Fondly do we hope—fervently do we pray—that this mighty scourge of war may speedily pass away.

Yet, if God wills that it continue, until all the wealth piled by the bondsman's two hundred and fifty years of unrequited toil shall be sunk, and until every drop of blood drawn with the lash, shall be paid by another drawn with the sword, as was said three thousand years ago, so still it must be said "the judgments of the Lord are true and righteous altogether."

With malice toward none; with charity for all; with firmness in the right as God gives us to see the right, let us strive on to finish the work we are in; to bind up the nation's wounds; to care for him who shall have borne the battle and for his widow and his orphan, to do all which may achieve and cherish a just, and lasting peace, among ourselves, and with all nations.

Consider the following theme's from Lincoln's *Second Inaugural Address:*

1. It may seem strange that any men should dare to ask a just God's assistance in wringing their bread from the sweat of other men's faces.

2. Woe unto the world because of offenses; for it must needs be that offenses come, but woe to that man by whom the offense cometh." If we shall suppose that American Slavery is one of those offenses which, in the providence of God, must needs come, but which, having continued through His appointed time, He now wills to remove, and that He gives to both North and South this terrible war, as the woe due to those by whom the offense came, shall we

discern therein any departure from those divine attributes which the believers in a living God always ascribe to Him? What appears Self-Evident is Lincoln's incredulity in the Confederacy's ability to invoke Divine Providence for the strength to continue the enslavement an oppression of one's fellow man. The willingness of the North to stay the course and lay down their lives and the lives of their brothers, fathers and sons in the name of overcoming the offense to Natural Law which was African Slavery, is indeed in the finest traditions of preserving, protecting and defending the Natural and equal rights of all men, and at extreme costs. A paradigm for all future generations to come.

To borrow once more from Lincoln, consider the following excerpt from his Gettysburg Address:

"...It is for us the living, rather, to be dedicated here to the unfinished work which they who fought here have thus far so nobly advanced. It is rather for us to be here dedicated to the great task remaining before us -- that from these honored dead we take increased devotion to that cause for which they gave the last full measure of devotion -- that we

here highly resolve that these dead shall not have died in vain -- that this nation, under God, shall have a new birth of freedom -- and that government of the people, by the people, for the people, shall not perish from the earth."

Summary - As we shall see in the forthcoming sections, *we the living*, all the generations of American's after the end of the American Civil War, have more often than not done a poor job in honoring those who gave their last full measure of devotion to a government of the people, by the people and for the people. The unfinished work left to do is to align the economic realities of 21st century America with the precepts of natural law, equality and justice and forever crush the dark thread of Machiavellian and Social Darwinistic philosophy which remain a modern scourge upon the people of this nation, and of the world. This will be accomplished by constructing new mechanisms which are firmly built upon the truth of interconnectivity and equitable service to one's fellow man and a dismantling of the process of egregious wealth accumulation as a function of the mindset of death and the desperate need to calm the chaos of that mindset with the delusion that monetized wealth produces harmony and artificially expands

errantly perceived finite time.

D. Robber Barons

The *Robber Barron* generation is that generation of industrialist that shaped the economic development of the United States after the Civil War. These men were acutely possessed of a philosophy of Social Darwinism and the righteousness of all means to wealth accumulation. This generation of men have a continuing and profound impact upon the culture of the United States in the 21st Century. They, in general represent the timeless image of "Success" in the mind of modern day Capitalistic America. To borrow from the Social Darwinists, these men are the most fit amongst us, this fitness is a function of their capacity to consolidate the power which arises from effectively and efficiently accumulating wealth.

This is a prevalent perspective in 21st century America. We continue to be a nation which colors wealth accumulation with the brush of righteousness and godliness and success, justified by the philosophies of Machiavelli and the Social Darwinists and the economic theory of Adam Smith.

It is essential here to align the behaviors of the Robber Barons with the most central meaning of sinfulness. As we have previously demonstrated here sin is a function of blindness to the truth of interconnectivity. The maniacal drive to create hyper stores of wealth is a direct function of the sinful, delusional and satanically deceived perspective of temporal scarcity. The false precept of temporal scarcity leads to its false extension into the concept of scarcity of economic resources as the production of economic resources are a function of temporal scarcity.

As was observed in the previous section, *"The willingness of the North to stay the course and lay down their lives as well as the lives of their brothers, fathers and sons in the name of overcoming the offense to Natural Law which was African Slavery is indeed in the finest tradition of preserving, protecting and defending the Natural and equal rights of all men, and at extreme costs. A paradigm for all future generations to come."* To extend this idea consider:

> *"...they did not love their lives so much as to shrink from death."*

222

In this context consider the contrast of that form of selfless sacrifice with the following. Just as the *Cornerstone Speech,* revealed and crystalized the heart and soul of the Confederacy, so to may the following reveal the heart and soul of the *Robber Barons* and therefore of Capitalists:

1.) *"John D. Rockefeller, a Cleveland, Ohio merchant, was also healthy and eligible to serve in the armed forces of the United States. He did not experience the Civil War in uniform. These men, and many others, avoided military service by simply taking advantage of that section of the Enrollment Act of 1863 allowing draftees to pay $300 to a substitute who served for them The enrollment list states that John W. Rockefeller was twenty-three years of age, a commercial merchant, and was born in New York. This parallels the events of John D. Rockefeller's life, for he was twenty-three at the time, having been born on July 8, 1839, in New York State. The Enrollment took place in June 1863. He was also a partner in the merchandising firm of Clark and Rockefeller, making him a "commercial* *merchant." Though a sense of uncertainty remains, the evidence is strong that this is John D. Rockefeller and that he purchased the services of a substitute." (Meier, 1994)*

2.) *"J. P. Morgan had started before the war, as the son of a banker who began selling stocks for the railroads for good commissions. During the Civil War he bought five thousand rifles for $3.50 each from an army arsenal, and sold them to a general in the field for $22 each. The rifles were defective and would shoot off the thumbs of the soldiers using them. A congressional committee noted this in the small print of an obscure report, but a federal judge upheld the deal as the fulfillment of a valid legal contract. Morgan had escaped military service in the Civil War by paying $300 to a substitute" (Zinn, n.d.)*

3.) *"...of Andrew Carnegie, the rail and steel magnate whose wealth was measured in billions. He paid a poor Irish immigrant the sum of $850 to fight in his place. He was but one of a number of rich men of his generation who would ultimately be referred to as "robber barons," since in addition to physically not serving, they would make money* *by providing the Union armies with everything that was needed, from uniforms and shoes to rifles" (Boltz 2014).*

4.) "Mellon's father had written to him that "a man may be a patriot without risking his own life or sacrificing his health. There are plenty of lives less valuable." (Zinn, n.d.).

As we will see in a later section of this work, the extreme wealth disparity in the United States of the 21st century is largely an extension of the lasting legacy and value systems exemplified by the Robber Barron generation. They in lock step and through their actions expressed the belief that the lives of men is distinguishable from one another as a function of the wealth they have accumulated. Mellon's observation that "a man may be a patriot without risking his own life or sacrificing his health, there are plenty of lives less valuable", clearly captures the ideals of these men. Cowardly, self-centered, and lustful of maximizing the accumulation of material wealth at the expense of the blood of true patriots, men willing to bleed to preserve and protect natural law, equality and justice. Their behaviors, to a man, represent an extreme application of the philosophies of Machiavelli and the

Social Darwinists and the economic theory of Adam Smith. These men indeed trafficked in the blood of their fellow men for their own obscene profit. These men have provided the model of American strength and success to be emulated, it is this dynamic that reinforces the disconnect between our modern economic system and the precepts of Locke which is the basis of our governmental system which is ostensibly founded upon the notions of the equality of all men and the protection and defense of natural rights among all people,

It is most useful, to consider that the soul of 21st Century America continues to be heavily shaped by the ideals of these men. Without clarity and intervention, the principles of the Constitution, the Declaration of Independence and the precepts of Natural Law as the basis of our society will remain impotent to overcome the current culture of death, war, greed and poverty whose foundation was set by the Robber Barons.

E. Stealing of the 1896 Presidential Election

The problems of 21st century America can be better understood through a careful reflection upon the circumstances surrounding the election of 1896. In many ways, the election of 1896 is a case study in shoring up the oligarchy's control over the resources of the republic and by extension their power to encroach upon the constitutional rights of all Americans. By reckless speculation in international commodities the Robber Barron generation induced the financial panic of 1893. This resulted in the failure of banks and a breakdown in the delivery of basic human services. As the Robber Barons controlled employment they were uniquely situated to tighten their grip upon the suffering American people whose labor barely provided them the means of survival and certainly not the resources needed to enjoy their constitutional rights. The value of their labor was consolidated in the hands of the wealthy and in times of induced financial panic such as both 1893 and 2008, the wealthy increase their illegal encroachment upon the constitutional rights of all Americans by destabilizing the conditions of labor and further consolidating their control of economic resources further deteriorating the practical ability of all Americans to enjoy their constitutional rights.

The poor, represented in what was referred to as the Populist Party sought financial market reforms which were theoretically designed to inflate the US Currency thereby decreasing the stranglehold that the debt of the poor had upon them. This would theoretically have had the effect of devaluing the holdings of the wealthy in favor of the masses. Consider the following excerpt from Howard Zinn's' *"A people' history of the United States 1492-2001"*

"In the election of 1896, with the Populist movement enticed into the Democratic party, Bryan, the Democratic candidate, was defeated by William McKinley, for whom the corporations and the press mobilized, in the first massive use of money in an election campaign. Even the hint of Populism in the Democratic Party, it seemed, could not be tolerated, and the big guns of the Establishment pulled out all their ammunition, to make sure. "

"It was a time, as election times have often been in the United States, to consolidate the system after years of protest and

rebellion. The black was being kept under control in the South.

The Indian was being driven off the western plains for good;

on a cold winter day in 1890, U.S. army soldiers attacked

Indians camped at Wounded Knee, South Dakota, and killed

three hundred men, women, and children. It was the climax to

four hundred years of violence that began with Columbus,

establishing that this continent belonged to white men. But only

to certain white men, because it was clear by 1896 that the state

stood ready to crush labor strikes, by the law if possible, by

force if necessary. And where a threatening mass movement

developed, the two-party system stood ready to send out one of

its columns to surround that movement and drain it of vitality."

"And always, as a way of drowning class resentment in a flood

of slogans for national unity, there was patriotism. McKinley

had said, in a rare rhetorical connection between money and

flag:

> *"... This year is going to be a year of patriotism and*
> *devotion to country. I am glad to know that the people in*
> *every part of the country mean to be devoted to one flag,*
> *the glorious Stars and Stripes; that the people of this*

229

country mean to maintain the financial honor of the country as sacredly as they maintain the honor of the flag."

"The supreme act of patriotism was war. Two years after McKinley became President, the United States declared war on Spain."

It may also be useful to demonstrate the effects that the hyper wealthy have upon American Culture. The Wizard of Oz, a popular work of children's literature, or at least ostensibly so, provided an allegorical representation of the circumstances of the nation at the time of the 1896 election, consider the following article from David Parker: *"The Rise and Fall of the Wizard of Oz as a parable on Populism (Parker, 1994)*

"The Wonderful Wizard of Oz is one of America's favorite pieces of juvenile literature. Children like it because it is a good story, full of fun characters and exciting adventures. Adults--especially those of us in history and related fields--like it because we can read between L. Frank Baum's lines and see various images of the United States at the turn of

the century. That has been true since 1964, when American Quarterly published Henry M. Littlefield's "The Wizard of Oz: Parable on Populism." Littlefield described all sorts of hidden meanings and allusions to Gilded Age society in The Wonderful Wizard of Oz: the wicked Witch of the East represented eastern industrialists and bankers who controlled the people (the Munchkins); the Scarecrow was the wise but naive western farmer; the Tin Woodman stood for the dehumanized industrial worker; the Cowardly Lion was William Jennings Bryan, Populist presidential candidate in 1896; the Yellow Brick Road, with all its dangers, was the gold standard; Dorothy's silver slippers (Judy Garland's were ruby red, but Baum originally made them silver) represented the Populists' solution to the nation's economic woes ("the free and unlimited coinage of silver"); Emerald City was Washington, D.C.; the Wizard, "a little bumbling old man, hiding behind a facade of paper mache and noise, . . . able to be everything to everybody," was any of the Gilded Age presidents."

Summary - The election of 1896 informs us that the direction of the United States is illegally determined upon the dictates of the wealthy. The use of stored wealth is mobilized to assure that when the excesses of reckless speculation result in the inevitable crash of financial markets that those with the capital needed to fund the electoral process see opportunity to increase the quotient of power their wealth exerts upon the American people, further encroaching upon the equal and just enjoyment of constitutional liberties in the name of further wealth consolidation in the hands of the hyper wealthy overlords of the American manor, whether it be the panic of 1893 or the crash of 2008.

F. Great Depression

To reiterate, the purpose of this text is to demonstrate that the nature of the universe is a cohesive singular field wrapped in paradox. Built upon this foundation of truth, logic proves out the fallacy of the economic precept of scarcity. The false notion of economic scarcity is a function of the false notion of temporal scarcity which has previously been demonstrated herein. It follows then that the philosophy of natural law, justice and equality need be not only the foundation of governmental systems but of economic systems as well. To continue to sustain economic systems built upon the false precepts of scarcity that lay at the foundation of Adam Smith's theory will serve to perpetuate the economic status quo which will continue a cycle of disharmony, chaos, war, crime and poverty.

The Machiavellian and Social Darwinistic philosophies of economic conservatives embrace the ideals of laissez-faire policies and trickledown theory. This always results in reckless unregulated speculation, the amplification of wealth consolidation and tremendous discontinuities which result in the disruption of balanced economic systems which facilitate the broad enjoyment of Natural Rights amongst all people.

The Great Depression illustrates and reinforces the truth that unregulated economic systems which are theoretically based upon the Social Darwinistic philosophies of Survival of the Fittest produce enormous human suffering, as these theories are based upon blindness to the true interconnected nature of the universe which as has been demonstrated here is a function of paradox or stated alternatively satanic deception.

Consider the following passage:

> *"...they have an unhealthy interest in controversies and quarrels about words that result in envy, strife, malicious talk, evil suspicions and constant friction between people of corrupt mind, who have been robbed of the truth and who think that godliness is a means to financial gain.*

> *"But godliness with contentment is great gain. For we brought nothing into the world, and we can take nothing out of it. But if we have food and clothing, we will be content with that. Those who want to get rich fall into temptation and*

a trap and into many foolish and harmful desires that plunge

people into ruin and destruction. For the love of money is a

root of all kinds of evil. Some people, eager for money, have

wandered from the faith and pierced themselves with many

griefs."

1 Timothy 6: 4-10

In 1 Timothy we are yet again reminded that people who orient their efforts toward becoming rich in possessions give birth to harmful desires that plunge people into ruin and destruction. An exceedingly accurate forecast as we examine the culture of America of the 1920s as a lead into the Great Depression.

Consider the following observations of Keynes:

"The outstanding faults of the economic society in which we

live are its failure to provide for full employment and its

arbitrary and inequitable distribution of wealth and

incomes."

"For my own part, I believe that there is social and

psychological justification for significant inequalities of

235

incomes and wealth, but not for such large disparities as exist today. There are valuable human activities which require the motive of money-making and the environment of private wealth-ownership for their full fruition. Moreover, dangerous human proclivities can be canalized into comparatively harmless channels by the existence of opportunities for money-making and private wealth, which, if they cannot be satisfied in this way, may find their outlet in cruelty, the reckless pursuit of personal power and authority, and other forms of self-aggrandizement. It is better that a man should tyrannize over his bank balance than over his fellow-citizens; and whilst the former is sometimes denounced as being but a means to the latter, sometimes at least it is an alternative. But it is not necessary for the stimulation of these activities and the satisfaction of these proclivities that the game should be played for such high stakes as at present. Much lower stakes will serve the purpose equally well, as soon as the players are accustomed to them. The task of transmuting human nature must not be confused with the task of managing it. Though in the ideal commonwealth men may have been taught or inspired or bred to take no interest in the stakes, it may still be wise and prudent statesmanship to allow the game to be played, subject to rules and limitations, so long as the average man, or even a significant section of the community, is in fact strongly addicted to the money-making passion."

The General Theory of Employment, Interest and Money
John Maynard Keynes
Chapter 24.
Concluding Notes on the Social Philosophy towards which the General Theory might Lead

Keynes clearly recognizes that the vast income and wealth disparities of his day are "the outstanding fault of the economic society". Further, he provides rationalization that within bounds there remains social and psychological justification for wealth disparity. He reasons, in the current era of men that it is better that the sociopathic personality be soothed through his lustful pursuit of wealth rather than to tyrannize his fellow man. In the very least Keynes helps us see that the personality type bent upon massive wealth accumulation is similar to those of more dangerous proclivities which drive men to tyrannize their fellow man. A clear description of the darkest characteristic amongst men.

The following analysis of the economic policies of the American Presidents of the 1920s has been retrieved from: http://www.digitalhistory.uh.edu/teachers/lesson_plans/pdfs/unit 9_1.pdf

"...there were few important differences between the conservative beliefs of Presidents Harding, Coolidge, and Hoover. Their ideas and policies therefore are summarized below:

Laissez-faire Policies

Conservatives believed that government should not interfere with the normal operations of the economy. Wages, prices, recessions, inflation, all these problems had a way of resolving themselves. The sum total of every person looking out for what is best for them or their business will result in what is best for everyone. If some businessmen were unsuccessful, or people ended up in poverty, 'not to worry'

— it was the natural order of things for the fittest to survive

and government should not interfere with the laws of nature. Examples of these ideas as they were carried out during the 1920's follow:

Veterans' bonuses

Soldiers who fought in World War I were paid only $16 a month. They would have made much more money if they stayed out of the army and continued their civilian jobs. They asked the government to pay them a bonus of $500 dollars, which they could collect when they retire in 1945 to make up for what they lost in their years of service. Harding, Coolidge, and Hoover opposed that plan.

Problems on America's farms

During World War I farmers expanded the size of their farms to produce food to help the allies. When the war ended in Europe food production soon returned to pre—war levels. Deprived of this market U.S. farmers were left with wheat, corn, and other products they could not sell. Because they had borrowed heavily during the war to keep up with *demand many farmers could not pay their debts. Banks started to call in farm loans and farmers often had no choice but sell their farms. Farmers led by Congressmen Charles McNary and Gilbert Haugen asked the Federal government to buy the surplus farm products and sell them at a loss to other countries. Liberals supported this plan but conservative presidents Harding, Coolidge, and Hoover opposed it.*

Laws regulating competition

Presidents Harding, Coolidge, and Hoover made few attempts to enforce laws against unfair competition, conspiracies to raise prices, and insider trading or similar practices in the stock market. Businessmen, in fact, were encouraged to plan together to avoid waste and unnecessary competition. Despite complaints by liberals the conservative Presidents during the 1920's practiced their laissez—faire beliefs regarding business regulation

Muscle Shoals Project

During World War I, the national government started building a dam at Muscles Shoals on the Tennessee River to make nitrates. These chemicals, used to manufacture explosives, could be used to make fertilizers. After the War, liberals thought the government should complete this dam. The power generated by the dam could be used to make inexpensive fertilizers and electricity for the people living in the area. Coolidge and Hoover opposed this plan. They wanted privately owned businesses, not the government, to build the dam and sell the electricity.

Trickle Down

Another fundamental belief of conservatives was the trickle down principle. They thought what was good for the wealthy and good for business would benefit the entire country because their money would trickle down to the poor in the form of jobs and opportunities to make money. Examples of these ideas as they were carried out during the 1920's follow

Tax reduction

The tax rate under the three conservative Presidents was reduced from 73% on the part of taxable incomes which exceed $1,000,000 (about 15 million, 1998 dollars) to 25% on such high incomes. These new rates saved Secretary of Treasury Andrew Mellon and his family about 2 million dollars a year. Not only were taxes for the rich reduced, money was paid back to businesses and people who had already paid their taxes under the old rates. Altogether $3.5 billion was handed back in this way.

Raising taxes on imports.

Conservatives raised tariffs shortly after World War I. The Fordney-McCumber Tariff under President Harding reversed the first major tariff reduction since the Civil War. The Hawley-Smoot tariff of 1931 under Herbert Hoover raised tariffs to an all-time high. It protected most businesses from all competition from foreign goods. These rate hikes were strongly opposed by liberals. As we have seen conservative policies from conservative presidents were based on a belief in laissez-faire and trickle down (Ladenberg 2007).

Yet again, we can clearly see that the economic policies of the conservative administrations of the *Roaring 20s,* founded upon the economic theory of Adam Smith and the philosophic justifications of the Social Darwinists inevitably leads to disharmony, chaos and human suffering.

Summary – The Great Depression serves as yet another reinforcement of the observation that a society that ostensibly orients is governmental system upon the righteous philosophies of John Locke and Thomas Jefferson while orienting its economic systems upon the errant economic theory of Adam Smith and the false philosophical system of the Social Darwinists will inevitably result in disequilibriums, volatility and great human suffering.

G.   King Capitalism and the War

American selflessness against the totalitarian and hateful tyranny of the Nazi's during World War II, reminds us of the reason for hope and certainty that the noble side of this nation will ultimately prevail in crushing the stranglehold that the economic theory of Adam Smith and the philosophical ideals of Machiavelli and the Social Darwinists has upon it. Notwithstanding, even at this time of noble self-sacrifice of most Americans, the dark specter of the satanic and paradoxical is present in the form of the war profiteers, in the mold of the *Robber Barons*. Consider the following excerpt from Franklin Delano Roosevelt's 1944 *State of the Union Address:*

> *"However, while the majority goes on about its great work without complaint, a noisy minority maintains an uproar of demands for special favors for special groups. There are pests who swarm through the lobbies of the Congress and the cocktail bars of Washington, representing these special groups as opposed to the basic interests of the Nation as a whole. They have come to look upon the war primarily as a chance to make profits for themselves at the expense of*

their neighbors, profits in money or in terms of political or social preferment. Such selfish agitation can be highly dangerous in wartime. It creates confusion. It damages morale. It hampers our national effort. It muddies the waters and therefore prolongs the war."

To further amplify the point, consider the following analysis of: *"Senator Harry S Truman and the Truman Committee Tackling war industry waste and worse"* (Zimmerman, 2012)

> *"On Dec. 21, 1942, the Justice Department issued an eight-count indictment against the Anaconda Wire and Cable Company and five of its employees, charging them with conspiracy to defraud the United States by supplying the Army and Navy with defective wire and cable intended for combat use and the billing of false expenses. It was, according to Attorney General Francis Biddle, "one of the most reprehensible cases of defrauding the government and endangering the lives of American soldiers and sailors ever to come to the attention of the Department of Justice."*
> *It was the latest example of action by the Senate Special*

Committee to Investigate the National Defense Program, more commonly known as the Truman Committee."

"In 1940 Congress authorized $10 billion to the U.S. military, enabling it to embark on the greatest expansion in its history. With the nation still recovering from the Great Depression, major corporations, seeing an opportunity to dramatically boost their bottom line, rushed to sign cost-plus military contracts. In 1941, Harry Truman, the junior senator from Missouri, began hearing reports of waste and profiteering in the construction of Fort Leonard Wood in his district. In typical fashion, the plain-spoken Truman decided to jump into his car and embark on a road trip to Fort Leonard Wood to see things for himself. In an age before the Interstate Highway system and over a road network composed of narrow two-lane highways, the senator wound up traveling about 10,000 miles, stopping at military installations from the Midwest to Florida. On Feb. 10, 1941, Senator Truman delivered a speech on the Senate floor describing the many problems he had seen and recommending that the Senate create a

special oversight committee on military contracts. As it turned out, his timing was perfect.

> *"I can conceive of nothing more vicious or treacherous than deliberately supplying our armed forces with defective war material. . . ."*

Attorney General Francis Biddle

"Pressure on the subject of federal waste and mismanagement in military spending had been building on the Roosevelt Administration from the beginning. When Rep. Edward Eugene Cox of Georgia, an anti-New Deal Democrat vocally joined with Republicans on the issue, President Franklin D. Roosevelt threw his support behind an investigative committee chaired by Truman, whom FDR viewed as a more practical alternative who would not go out of his way to embarrass the administration. On March 1, 1941, by unanimous vote, the Senate approved the oversight committee with Truman as its chairman. With the exception of Army Chief of Staff Gen. George C. Marshall, senior military leaders were worried. Past experience with

247

similar committees during the Civil War and immediately following World War I had not been good. The Union's Joint Committee on the Conduct of the War had been so meddlesome and harassing that Gen. Robert E. Lee joked it was worth two divisions to the Confederacy. Marshall, on the other hand, reassured his peers that "members of Congress are just as patriotic as we are."

"Truman selected the members for his committee from both aisles, more concerned about the individual being fair and pragmatic rather which party he was a member. Truman moved quickly, initially focusing on construction cost overruns at Army facilities. His committee's investigation revealed much waste and cronyism and led to responsibility being transferred from the Quartermaster Corps to that of the Corps of Engineers, ultimately saving the government $250 million. That success caused Congress to increase the committee's budget and staff, enabling it to expand its investigations."

"The Anaconda wire fraud case amounted to $6 million in defective wire and cable being sold to the United States government. Lend-Lease shipments of the Anaconda products to the Soviet Union were 50 percent defective, causing the Soviet government to file an official protest."

"In the summer of 1943, the Truman Committee revealed that the Lockland, Ohio, plant of the Curtiss-Wright company had been supplying defective aircraft engines to the Army Air Force; charges included conspiracy and collusion with AAF inspectors. This scandal became an inspiration for playwright Arthur Miller's play All My Sons."

"Truman's success in curbing profiteering and mismanagement and helping to indict offenders gained Truman a respected national reputation. Typical was a letter from L.E. Hudson of Tulsa, Okla., who wrote on Oct. 9, 1943, "You and your committee have done and are doing a great good and we folks who have sons in the

service can't thank you enough for the work you have done."

"Truman stepped down from the committee in 1944, when he became FDR's vice presidential running mate. The Truman Committee would continue until 1948, proving to be one of the most successful investigative committees created by Congress, saving the government an estimated $15 billion and the lives of thousands of servicemen."

As was the case with Lincoln during the Civil War, so to with FDR during World War II whereby the President recognized the true noble essence of a nation of the people, by the people and for the people, when called upon to sacrifice for the specific purpose of defending the natural rights, equality and justice, not only for themselves but for others. Consider the following transcript of FDR's fireside chat, April 28, 1942 (retrieved, January 19, 2016 from: http://legacy.fordham.edu/halsall/mod/1942roosevelt-sacrifice.html

"My Fellow Americans, it is nearly five months since we were attacked at Pearl Harbor. For the two years prior to

that attack this country had been gearing itself up to a high level of production of munitions. And yet our war efforts had done little to dislocate the normal lives of most of us. Since then we have dispatched strong forces of our Army and Navy, several hundred thousands of them, to bases and battlefronts thousands of miles from home. We have stepped up our war production on a scale that is testing our industrial power, our engineering genius, and our economic structure to the utmost. We have had no illusions about the fact that this is a tough job-and a long one. American warships are now in combat in the North and South Atlantic, in the Arctic, in the Mediterranean, in the Indian Ocean, and in the North and South Pacific. American troops have taken stations in South America, Greenland, Iceland, the British Isles, the Near East, the Middle East and the Far East, the continent of Australia, and many islands of the Pacific. American war planes, manned by Americans, are flying in actual combat over all the continents and all the oceans.

On the European front the most important development of the past year has been without question the crushing counteroffensive on the part of the great armies of Russia against the powerful German army. These Russian forces have destroyed and are destroying more armed power of our enemies-troops, planes, tanks, and guns-than all the other United Nations put together. In the Mediterranean area, matters remain on the surface much as they were. But the situation there is receiving very careful attention. Recently, we've received news of a change in government in what we used to know as the Republic of France-a name dear to the hearts of all lovers of liberty, a name and an institution which we hope will soon be restored to full dignity. Throughout the Nazi occupation of France, we have hoped for the maintenance of a French government which would strive to regain independence, to reestablish the principles of "Liberty, Equality, and Fraternity," and to restore the historic culture of France. Our policy has been consistent from the very beginning. However, we are now greatly concerned lest those who have recently come to power may seek to force the brave French people into submission to Nazi despotism. The United Nations will take measures, if necessary, to prevent the use of French territory in any part of the world for military purposes by the Axis powers. The good people of France will readily understand that such action is essential for the United Nations to prevent assistance to the armies or navies or air forces of Germany or Italy or Japan. The overwhelming majority of the French people understand that the fight of the United Nations is fundamentally their fight, that our victory means the restoration of a free and independent France-and the saving of France from the slavery which would be imposed upon her by her external enemies and by her internal traitors.

We know how the French people really feel. We know that a deep-seated determination to obstruct every step in the Axis plan extends from occupied France through Vichy France all the way to the people of their colonies in every ocean and on every continent. Our planes are helping in the defense of French colonies today, and soon American Flying Fortresses will be fighting for the liberation of the darkened continent of Europe itself. In all the occupied countries there are men and women, and even little children, who have never stopped fighting, never stopped resisting, never stopped proving to the Nazis that their so-called new order will never be enforced upon free peoples. In the German and Italian peoples themselves there's a growing conviction that the cause of Nazism and Fascism is hopeless-that their political and military leaders have led them along the bitter road which leads not to world conquest but to final defeat. They cannot fail to contrast the present frantic speeches of these leaders with their arrogant boastings of a year ago, and two years ago. And on the other side of the world, in the Far East, we have passed through a phase of serious losses. We have inevitably lost control of a large portion of the Philippine Islands. But this whole nation pays tribute to the Filipino and American officers and men who held out so long on Bataan Peninsula, to those grim and gallant fighters who still hold Corregidor, where the flag flies, and to the forces that are still striking effectively at the enemy on Mindanao and other islands. The Malayan Peninsula and Singapore are in the hands of the enemy; the Netherlands East Indies are almost entirely occupied, though resistance there continues. Many other islands are in the possession of the Japanese. But there is good reason to believe that their southward advance has been checked. Australia, New Zealand, and much other territory will be bases for offensive action-and we are determined that the territory that has been lost will be regained.

The Japanese are pressing their northward advance against Burma with considerable power, driving toward India and China. They have been opposed with great bravery by small British and Chinese forces aided by American fliers. The news in Burma tonight is not good. The Japanese may cut the Burma Road; but I want to say to the gallant people of China that no matter what advances the Japanese may make, ways will be found to deliver airplanes and munitions of war to the armies of Generalissimo Chiang Kai-shek. We remember that the Chinese people were the first to stand up and fight against the aggressors in this war; and in the future a still unconquerable China will play its proper role in maintaining peace and prosperity, not only in eastern Asia but in the whole world. For every advance that the Japanese have made since they started their frenzied career of conquest, they have had to pay a very heavy toll in warships, in transports, in planes, and in men. They are feeling the effects of those losses.

It is even reported from Japan that somebody has dropped bombs on Tokyo, and on other principal centers of Japanese war industries. If this be true, it is the first time in history that Japan has suffered such indignities' although the treacherous attack on Pearl Harbor was the immediate cause of our entry into the war, that event found the American people spiritually prepared for war on a worldwide scale. We went into this war fighting. We know what we are fighting for, we realize that the war has become what Hitler originally proclaimed it to be-a total war. Not all of us can have the privilege of fighting our enemies in distant parts of the world. Not all of us can have the privilege of working in a munitions factory or a shipyard, or on the farms or in oil fields or mines, producing the weapons or the raw materials that are needed by our armed forces. But there is one front and one battle where everyone in the United States-every man, woman, and child-is in action, and will be privileged to remain in action throughout this war. That front is right here at home, in our daily lives, in our daily tasks. Here at home everyone will have the privilege of making whatever self-denial is necessary, not only to supply our fighting men, but to keep the economic structure of our country fortified and secure during the war and after the war. This will require, of course, the abandonment not only of luxuries but of many other creature comforts. Every loyal American is aware of his individual responsibility. Whenever I hear anyone saying, "The American people are complacent-they need to be aroused," I feel like asking him to come to Washington to read the mail that floods into the White House and into all departments of this government. The one question that recurs through all these thousands of letters and messages is, "What more can I do to help my country in winning this war?"

To build the factories, to buy the materials, to pay the labor, to provide the transportation, to equip and feed and house the soldiers and sailors and marines, and to do all the thousands of things necessary in a war-all cost a lot of money, more money than has ever been spent by any nation at anytime in the long history of the world. We are now spending, solely for war purposes, the sum of about $100 million every day in the week. But, before this year is over, that almost unbelievable rate of expenditure will be doubled. All of this money has to be spent-and spent quickly-if we are to produce within the time now available the enormous quantities of weapons of war which we need. But the spending of these tremendous sums presents grave danger of disaster to our national economy. When your government continues to spend these unprecedented sums for munitions month by month and year by year, that money goes into the pocketbooks and bank accounts of the people of the United States. At the same time raw materials and many manufactured goods are necessarily taken away from civilian use; and machinery and factories are being converted to war production. You do not have to be a *professor of mathematics or economics to see that if people*

with plenty of cash start bidding against each other for

scarce goods, the price of those goods goes up. Yesterday

I submitted to the Congress of the United States a seven-

point program, a program of general principles which

taken together could be called the national economic

policy for attaining the great objective of keeping the cost

of living down. I repeat them now to you in substance:

First, we must, through heavier taxes, keep personal and

corporate profits at a low reasonable rate. Second, we

must fix ceilings on prices and rents. Third, we must

stabilize wages. Fourth, we must stabilize farm prices.

Fifth, we must put more billions into war bonds. Sixth, we

must ration all essential commodities which are scarce.

And seventh, we must discourage installment buying, and

encourage paying off debts and mortgages.

I do not think it is necessary to repeat what I said yesterday

to the Congress in discussing these general principles. The

important thing to remember is that each one of these

points is dependent on the others if the whole program is

to work. Some people are already taking the position that every one of the seven points is correct except the one point which steps on their own individual toes. A few seem very willing to approve self-denial - on the part of their neighbors. The only effective course of action is a simultaneous attack on all of the factors which increase the cost of living, in one comprehensive, all embracing program covering prices and profits and wages and taxes and debts. The blunt fact is that every single person in the United States is going to be affected by this program. Some of you will be affected more directly by one or two of these restrictive measures, but all of you will be affected indirectly by all of them. Are you a businessman, or do you own stock in a business corporation? Well, your profits are going to be cut down to a reasonably low level by taxation. Your income will be subject to higher taxes. Indeed in these days, when every available dollar should go to the war effort, I do not think that any American citizen should have a net income in excess of $25,000 per year after payment of taxes. Are you a retailer or a wholesaler or a manufacturer or a farmer or a landlord? Ceilings are *being placed on the prices at which you can sell your goods or rent your property. Do you work for wages? You will have to forgo higher wages for your particular job for the duration of the war.*

All of us are used to spending money for things that we want, things, however, which are not absolutely essential. We will all have to forgo that kind of spending. Because we must put every dime and every dollar we can possibly spare out of our earnings into war bonds and stamps. Because the demands of the war effort require the rationing of goods of which there is not enough to go around. Because the stopping of purchases of nonessentials will release thousands of workers who are needed in the war effort. As I told the Congress yesterday, "sacrifice" is not exactly the proper word with which to describe this program of self-denial. When, at the end of this great struggle, we shall have saved our free way of life, we shall have made no "sacrifice." The price for civilization must be paid in hard work and sorrow and blood. The price is not too high. If you doubt it, ask those millions who live today under the tyranny of Hitlerism.

Ask the workers of France and Norway and the Netherlands, whipped to labor by the lash, whether the stabilization of wages is too great a "sacrifice." Ask the farmers of Poland and Denmark and Czechoslovakia and France, looted of their livestock, starving while their own crops are stolen from their land, ask them whether parity prices are too great a sacrifice." Ask the businessmen of Europe, whose enterprises have been stolen from their owners, whether the limitation of profits and personal incomes is too great a "sacrifice." Ask the women and children whom Hitler is starving whether the rationing of tires and gasoline and sugar is too great a "sacrifice." We do not have to ask them. They have already given us their agonized answers.

This Great War effort must be carried through to its victorious conclusion by the indomitable will and determination of the people as one great whole. It must not be impeded by the faint of heart. It must not be impeded by those who put their own selfish interests above the interests

of the nation. It must not be impeded by those who pervert

honest criticism into falsification of fact. It must not be

impeded by self-styled experts either in economics or

military problems who know neither true figures nor

geography itself. It must not be impeded by a few bogus

patriots who use the sacred freedom of the press to echo

the sentiments of the propagandists in Tokyo and Berlin.

And, above all, it shall not be imperiled by the handful of

noisy traitors - betrayers of America, betrayers of

Christianity itself - would-be dictators who in their hearts

and souls have yielded to Hitlerism and would have this

republic do likewise. I shall use all of the executive power

that I have to carry out the policy laid down. If it becomes

necessary to ask for any additional legislation in order to

attain our objective of preventing a spiral in the cost of

living, I shall do so.

I know the American farmer, the American workman, and

the American businessman. I know that they will gladly

embrace this economy and equality of sacrifice-satisfied

that it is necessary for the most vital and compelling motive in all their lives-winning through to victory. Never in the memory of man has there been a war in which the courage, the endurance, and the loyalty of civilians played so vital a part. Many thousands of civilians all over the world have been and are being killed or maimed by enemy action. Indeed, it is the fortitude of the common people of Britain under fire which enabled that island to stand and prevented Hitler from winning the war in 1940. The ruins of London and Coventry and other cities are today the proudest monuments to British heroism. Our own American civilian population is now relatively safe from such disasters. And, to an ever increasing extent, our soldiers, sailors, and marines are fighting with great bravery and great skills on far distant fronts to make sure that we shall remain safe. I should like to tell you one or two stories about the men we have in our armed forces: There is, for example, Dr. Corydon M. Wassell. He was a missionary, well known for his good works in China. He is a simple, modest, retiring man, nearly sixty years old, but he entered the service of his country and was commissioned a lieutenant commander in the navy. Dr. Wassell was assigned to duty in Java caring for wounded officers and men of the cruisers Houston and Marblehead which had been in heavy action in the Java seas. When the Japanese advanced across the island, it was decided to evacuate as many as possible of the wounded to Australia. But about twelve of the men were so badly wounded that they couldn't be moved. Dr. Wassell remained with them, knowing that he would be captured by the enemy. But he decided to make a last desperate attempt to get the men out of Java. He asked each of them if he wished to take the chance, and everyone agreed. He first had to get the twelve men to the seacoast-fifty miles away. To do this, he had to improvise stretchers for the hazardous journey. The men were suffering severely, but Dr. Wassell kept them alive by his skill, inspired them by his own courage. And as the official report said, Dr. Wassell was "almost like a Christ-like shepherd devoted to his flock." On the seacoast, he embarked the men on a little Dutch ship. They were bombed, they were machinegunned by waves of Japanese planes. Dr. Wassell took virtual command of the ship, and by great skill avoided destruction, hiding in little bays and little inlets. A few days later, Dr. Wassell and his small flock of wounded men reached Australia safely. And today Dr. Wassell wears the Navy Cross.

Another story concerns a ship, a ship rather than an individual man. You may remember the tragic sinking of the submarine, the United States Ship Squalus, off the New England coast in the summer of 1939. Some of the crew were lost, but others were saved by the speed and the efficiency of the surface rescue crews. The Squalus itself was tediously raised from the bottom of the sea. She was repaired, put back into commission, and eventually she sailed again under a new name, the United States Ship Sailfish. Today, she is a potent and effective unit of our submarine fleet in the Southwest Pacific. The Sailfish has covered many thousands of miles in operations in those far waters. She has sunk a Japanese destroyer. She has torpedoed a Japanese cruiser. She has made torpedo hits-two of them-on a Japanese aircraft carrier. Three of the enlisted men of our Navy who went down with the Squalus in 1939 and were rescued are today serving on the same ship, the United States Ship Sailfish, in this war. It seems to me that it is heartening to know that the Squalus, once given up as lost, rose from the depths to fight for our country in time of peril. One more story that I heard only this morning. This a story of one of our Army Flying Fortresses operating in the western Pacific. The pilot of this plane is a modest young man, proud of his crew for one of the toughest fights a bomber has yet experienced. The bomber departed from its base, as part of a flight of five bombers, to attack Japanese transports that were landing troops against us in the Philippines. When they had gone about halfway to their destination, one of the motors of this bomber went out of commission. The young pilot lost contact with the other bombers. The crew, however, got the motor working, got it going again and the plane proceeded on its mission alone. By the time it arrived at its target the other four Flying Fortresses had already passed over, had dropped their bombs, and had stirred up the hornets' nest of Japanese "Zero" planes. Eighteen of these Zero fighters attacked our one Flying Fortress.

267

Despite this mass attack, our plane proceeded on its mission, and dropped all of its bombs on six Japanese transports which were lined up along the docks. As it turned back on its homeward journey a running fight between the bomber and the eighteen Japanese pursuit planes continued for seventy-five miles. Four pursuit planes of the Japs attacked simultaneously at each side. Four were shot down with the side guns. During this fight, the bomber's radio operator was killed, the engineer's right hand was shot off, and one gunner was crippled, leaving only one man available to operate both side guns. Although wounded in one hand, this gunner alternately manned both side guns, bringing down three more Japanese Zero planes. While this was going on, one engine on the American bomber was shot out, one gas tank was hit, the radio was shot off, and the oxygen system was entirely destroyed. Out of eleven control cables all but four were shot away. The rear landing wheel was blown off entirely, and the two front wheels were both shot flat.

The fight continued until the remaining Japanese pursuit ships exhausted their ammunition and turned back. With two engines gone and the plane practically out of control, the American bomber returned to its base after dark and made an emergency landing. The mission had been accomplished. The name of that pilot is Captain Hewitt T. Wheless, of the United States Army. He comes from a place called Menard, Texas-with a population of 2,375. He has been awarded the Distinguished Service Cross. And I hope that he is listening. These stories I have told you are not exceptional. They are typical examples of individual heroism and skill. As we here at home contemplate our own duties, our own responsibilities, let us think and think hard of the example which is being set for us by our fighting men. Our soldiers and sailors are members of well-disciplined units. But they're still and forever individuals free individuals. They are farmers and workers, businessmen, professional men, artists, clerks. They are the United States of America. That is why they fight. We too are the United States of America. That is why we must work and sacrifice. It is for them. It is for us. It is for victory.

The above transcript provides the entirety of this *Fireside Chat*. The relevance within the context of this work is the basis of FDR's sentiment regarding the finest aspects of America as a clear manifestation of a mindset of self-sacrifice as evidence of an intuitive embracing of universal interconnectivity, in contrast to the satanic and paradoxical aspects represented by the behaviors of the war profiteers. The following excerpt brings focused attention to this notion:

> *"I know the American farmer, the American workman, and the American businessman. I know that they will gladly embrace this economy and equality of sacrifice-satisfied that it is necessary for the most vital and compelling motive in all their lives-winning through to victory. Never in the memory of man has there been a war in which the courage, the endurance, and the loyalty of civilians played so vital a part. Many thousands of civilians all over the world have been and are being killed or maimed by enemy action. Indeed, it is the fortitude of the common people of*

Britain under fire which enabled that island to stand and prevented Hitler from winning the war in 1940. The ruins of London and Coventry and other cities are today the proudest monuments to British heroism"

Again, just as had been observed during the Civil War, true patriots of a government of the people, by the people and for the people, founded upon the precepts of Natural Law, equality and justice, are often willing to sacrifice greatly, often to the last full measure of devotion, to preserve, protect and defend these ideals, not only for their families and nation but for others in foreign lands under the lash of tyranny.

Summary – The purpose of this section is to highlight, that even in times of great national peril, the dark shadow of the economic theory of Adam Smith and the philosophies of the Machiavelli and the Social Darwinists manifest in the behaviors of the most self-centered and greedy among us. It is relevant to see this dynamic as it the very same dynamic at work in 21st century America which has resulted in a wealth distribution paradigm that negates the practical enjoyment of natural rights by the vast majority of American society.

H. Evaporation of FDRs post war Economic Bill of Rights

As a function of having navigated the United States through the Great Depression from 1932 -1941, and then leading this nation of the people, by the people and for the people, FDR knew with certainty what post-war America ought to strive to become. His blueprint for post-war America is embedded in his 1944 State of the Union Address. The following transcript was retrieved on January 23, 2016 from:

http://www.presidency.ucsb.edu/ws/?pid=16518

> *To the Congress:*
>
> *This Nation in the past two years has become an active partner in the world's greatest war against human slavery. We have joined with like-minded people in order to defend ourselves in a world that has been gravely threatened with gangster rule. But I do not think that any of us Americans can be content with mere survival. Sacrifices that we and our allies are making impose upon us all a sacred obligation to see to it that out of this war we and our children will gain something better than mere survival. We are united in determination that this war shall not be*

followed by another interim which leads to new disaster—that we shall not repeat the tragic errors of ostrich isolationism—that we shall not repeat the excesses of the wild twenties when this Nation went for a joy ride on a roller coaster which ended in a tragic crash.

When Mr. Hull went to Moscow in October, and when I went to Cairo and Teheran in November, we knew that we were in agreement with our allies in our common determination to fight and win this war. But there were many vital questions concerning the future peace, and they were discussed in an atmosphere of complete candor and harmony. In the last war such discussions, such meetings, did not even begin until the shooting had stopped and the delegates began to assemble at the peace table. There had been no previous opportunities for man-to-man discussions which lead to meetings of minds. The result was a peace which was not a peace. That was a mistake which we are not repeating in this war. And right here I want to address a word or two to some suspicious souls who are fearful that Mr. Hull or I have made "commitments" for the future which might pledge this Nation to secret treaties, or to enacting the role of Santa Claus. To such suspicious souls—using a polite terminology—I wish to say that Mr. Churchill, and Marshal Stalin, and Generalissimo Chiang Kai-shek are all thoroughly conversant with the provisions of our Constitution. And so is Mr. Hull. And so am I. Of course we made some commitments. We most certainly committed ourselves to very large and very specific military plans which require the use of all Allied forces to bring about the defeat of our enemies at the earliest possible time. But there were no secret treaties or political or financial commitments.

The one supreme objective for the future, which we discussed for each Nation individually, and for all the United Nations, can be summed up in one word: Security. And that means not only physical security which provides safety from attacks by aggressors. It means also economic security, social security, moral security—in a family of Nations. In the plain down-to-earth talks that I had with the Generalissimo and Marshal

Stalin and Prime Minister Churchill, it was abundantly clear that they are all most deeply interested in the resumption of peaceful progress by their own peoples—progress toward a better life. All our allies want freedom to develop their lands and resources, to build up industry, to increase education and individual opportunity, and to raise standards of living. All our allies have learned by bitter experience that real development will not be possible if they are to be diverted from their purpose by repeated wars—or even threats of war. China and Russia are truly united with Britain and America in recognition of this essential fact: The best interests of each Nation, large and small, demand that all freedom-loving Nations shall join together in a just and durable system of peace. In the present world situation, evidenced by the actions of Germany, Italy, and Japan, unquestioned military control over disturbers of the peace is as necessary among Nations as it is among citizens in a community. And an equally basic essential to peace is a decent standard of living for all individual men and women and children in all Nations.

Freedom from fear is eternally linked with freedom from want.

There are people who burrow through our Nation like unseeing moles, and attempt to spread the suspicion that if other Nations are encouraged to raise their standards of living, our own American standard of living must of necessity be depressed. The fact is the very contrary. It has been shown time and again that if the standard of living of any country goes up, so does its purchasing power- and that such a rise encourages a better standard of living in neighboring countries with whom it trades. That is just plain common sense—and it is the kind of plain common sense that provided the basis for our discussions at Moscow, Cairo, and Teheran.

Returning from my journeyings, I must confess to a sense of "let-down" when I found many evidences of faulty perspective here in Washington. The faulty perspective consists in overemphasizing lesser problems and thereby underemphasizing the first and greatest problem. The overwhelming majority of our people have met the demands of this war with magnificent courage and understanding. They have accepted inconveniences; they have accepted hardships; they have accepted tragic sacrifices. And they are ready and eager to make whatever further contributions are needed to win the war as quickly as possible- if only they are given the chance to know what is required of them. However, while the majority goes on about its great work without complaint, a noisy minority maintains an uproar of demands for special favors for special groups. There are pests who swarm through the lobbies of the Congress and the cocktail bars of Washington, representing these special groups as opposed to the basic interests of the Nation as a whole. They have come to look upon the war primarily as a chance to make profits for themselves at the expense of their neighbors- profits in money or in terms of political or social preferment. Such selfish agitation can be highly dangerous in wartime. It creates confusion. It damages morale. It hampers our national effort. It muddies the waters and therefore prolongs the war.

If we analyze American history impartially, we cannot escape the fact that in our past we have not always forgotten individual and selfish and partisan interests in time of war—we have not always been united in purpose and direction. We cannot overlook the serious dissensions and the lack of unity in our war of the Revolution, in our War of 1812, or in our War Between the States, when the survival of the Union itself was at stake. In the first World War we came closer to national unity than in any previous war. But that war lasted only a year and a half, and increasing signs of disunity began to appear during the final months of the conflict. In this war, we have been compelled to learn how interdependent upon each other are all groups and sections of the population of America. Increased food costs, for example, will bring new demands for wage increases from all war workers, which will in turn raise all prices of all things including those things which the farmers themselves have to buy. Increased wages or prices will each in turn produce the same results. They all have a particularly disastrous result on all fixed income groups. And I hope you will remember that all of us in this Government represent the fixed income group just as much as we represent business owners, workers, and farmers. This group of fixed income people includes: teachers, clergy, policemen, firemen, widows and minors on fixed incomes, wives and dependents of our soldiers and sailors, and old-age pensioners. They and their families add up to one-quarter of our one hundred and thirty million people. They have few or no high pressure representatives at the Capitol. In a period of gross inflation they would be the worst sufferers. If ever there was a time to subordinate individual or group selfishness to the national good, that time is now. Disunity at home—bickerings, self-seeking partisanship, stoppages of work, inflation, business as usual, politics as usual, luxury as usual these are the influences which can undermine the morale of the brave men ready to die at the front for us here. Those who are doing most of the complaining are not deliberately striving to sabotage the national war effort. They are laboring under the delusion that the time is past when we must make prodigious sacrifices- that the war is already won and we can begin to slacken off. But the dangerous folly of that point of view can be measured by the distance that separates our troops from their ultimate objectives in Berlin and Tokyo—and by the sum of all the perils that lie along the way.

Overconfidence and complacency are among our deadliest enemies. Last spring—after notable victories at Stalingrad and in Tunisia and against the U-boats on the high seas— overconfidence became so pronounced that war production fell off. In two months, June and July, 1943, more than a thousand airplanes that could have been made and should have been made were not made. Those who failed to make them were not on strike. They were merely saying, "The war's in the bag- so let's relax." That attitude on the part of anyone—Government or management or labor—can lengthen this war. It can kill American boys. Let us remember the lessons of 1918. In the summer of that year the tide turned in favor of the allies. But this Government did not relax. In fact, our national effort was stepped up. In August, 1918, the draft age limits were broadened from 21-31 to 18-45. The President called for "force to the utmost," and his call was heeded. And in November, only three months later, Germany surrendered. That is the way to fight and win a war—all out—and not with half-an-eye on the battlefronts abroad and the other eye-and-a-half on personal, selfish, or political interests here at home. Therefore, in order to concentrate all our energies and resources on winning the war, and to maintain a fair and stable economy at home, I recommend that the Congress adopt:

(1) A realistic tax law—which will tax all unreasonable profits, both individual and corporate, and reduce the ultimate cost of the war to our sons and daughters. The tax bill now under consideration by the Congress does not begin to meet this test.

(2) A continuation of the law for the renegotiation of war contracts— which will prevent exorbitant profits and assure fair prices to the Government. For two long years I have pleaded with the Congress to take undue profits out of war.

(3) A cost of food law—which will enable the Government (a) to place a reasonable floor under the prices the farmer may expect for his production; and (b) to place a ceiling on the prices a

consumer will have to pay for the food he buys. This should apply to necessities only; and will require public funds to carry out. It will cost in appropriations about one percent of the present annual cost of the war.

(4) Early reenactment of. The stabilization statute of October, 1942. This expires June 30, 1944, and if it is not extended well in advance, the country might just as well expect price chaos by summer. We cannot have stabilization by wishful thinking. We must take positive action to maintain the integrity of the American dollar.

(5) A national service law- which, for the duration of the war, will prevent strikes, and, with certain appropriate exceptions, will make available for war production or for any other essential services every able-bodied adult in this Nation.

These five measures together form a just and equitable whole. I would not recommend a national service law unless the other laws were passed to keep down the cost of living, to share equitably the burdens of taxation, to hold the stabilization line, and to prevent undue profits. The Federal Government already has the basic power to draft capital and property of all kinds for war purposes on a basis of just compensation. As you know, I have for three years hesitated to recommend a national service act. Today, however, I am convinced of its necessity. Although I believe that we and our allies can win the war without such a measure, I am certain that nothing less than total mobilization of all our resources of manpower and capital will guarantee an earlier victory, and reduce the toll of suffering and sorrow and blood. I have received a joint recommendation for this law from the heads of the War Department, the Navy Department, and the Maritime Commission. These are the men who bear responsibility for the procurement of the necessary arms and equipment, and for the successful prosecution of the war in the field. They say:

"When the very life of the Nation is in peril the responsibility for service is common to all men and women. In such a time there can be no discrimination between the men and women who are assigned by the Government to its defense at the battlefront and the men and women assigned to producing the vital materials essential to successful military operations. A prompt enactment of

a National Service Law would be merely an expression of the universality of this responsibility."

I believe the country will agree that those statements are the solemn truth. National service is the most democratic way to wage a war. Like selective service for the armed forces, it rests on the obligation of each citizen to serve his Nation to his utmost where he is best qualified. It does not mean reduction in wages. It does not mean loss of retirement and seniority rights and benefits. It does not mean that any substantial numbers of war workers will be disturbed in their present jobs. Let these facts be wholly clear. Experience in other democratic Nations at war—Britain, Canada, Australia, and New Zealand- has shown that the very existence of national service makes unnecessary the widespread use of compulsory power. National service has proven to be a unifying moral force based on an equal and comprehensive legal obligation of all people in a Nation at war. There are millions of American men and women who are not in this war at all. It is not because they do not want to be in it. But they want to know where they can best do their share. National service provides that direction. It will be a means by which every man and woman can find that inner satisfaction which comes from making the fullest possible contribution to victory. I know that all civilian war workers will be glad to be able to say many years hence to their grandchildren: "Yes, I, too, was in service in the great war. I was on duty in an airplane factory, and I helped make hundreds of fighting planes. The Government told me that in doing that I was performing my most useful work in the service of my country." It is argued that we have passed the stage in the war where national service is necessary. But our soldiers and sailors know that this is not true. We are going forward on a long, rough road- and, in all journeys, the last miles are the hardest. And it is for that final effort—for the total defeat of our enemies-that we must mobilize our total resources. The national war program calls for the employment of more people in 1944 than in 1943. It is my conviction that the American people will welcome this win-the-war measure which is based on the eternally just principle of "fair for one, fair for all." It will give our people at home the assurance that they are standing four-square behind our soldiers and sailors. And it will give our enemies demoralizing assurance that we mean business that we, 130,000,000 Americans, are on the march to Rome, Berlin, and Tokyo. I hope that the Congress will recognize that, although this is a political year, national service is an issue which transcends politics. Great power must be used for great purposes. As to the machinery for this measure, the Congress itself should determine its nature—but it should be wholly nonpartisan in its make-up. Our armed forces are valiantly fulfilling their responsibilities to our country and our people. Now the Congress faces the responsibility for taking those measures which are essential to national security in this the most decisive phase of the Nation's greatest war. Several alleged reasons have prevented the enactment of legislation which would preserve for our soldiers and sailors and marines the fundamental prerogative of citizenship—the right to vote. No amount of legalistic argument can becloud this issue in the eyes of these ten million American citizens. Surely the signers of the Constitution did not intend a document which, even in wartime, would be construed to take away the franchise of any of those who are fighting to preserve the Constitution itself. Our soldiers and sailors and marines know that the overwhelming majority of them will be deprived of the opportunity to vote, if the voting machinery is left exclusively to the States under existing State laws—and that there is no likelihood of these laws being changed in time to enable them to vote at the next election. The Army and Navy have reported that it will be impossible effectively to administer forty-eight different soldier voting laws. It is the duty of the Congress to remove this unjustifiable discrimination against the men and women in our armed forces- and to do it as quickly as possible.

It is our duty now to begin to lay the plans and determine the strategy for the winning of a lasting peace and the establishment of an American standard of living higher than ever before known. We cannot be content, no matter how high that general standard of living may be, if some fraction of our people—whether it be one-third or one-fifth or one-tenth- is ill-fed, ill-clothed, ill housed, and insecure. This Republic had its beginning, and grew to its present strength, under the protection of certain inalienable political rights—among them the right of free speech, free press, free worship, trial by jury, freedom from unreasonable searches and seizures. They were our rights to life and liberty. As our

Nation has grown in size and stature, however—as our industrial economy expanded—these political rights proved inadequate to assure us equality in the pursuit of happiness. We have come to a clear realization of the fact that true individual freedom cannot exist without economic security and independence. "Necessitous men are not free men." People who are hungry and out of a job are the stuff of which dictatorships are made In our day these economic truths have become accepted as self-evident. We have accepted, so to speak, a second Bill of Rights under which a new basis of security and prosperity can be established for all regardless of station, race, or creed.

Among these are:

> *The right to a useful and remunerative job in the industries or shops or farms or mines of the Nation;*

> *The right to earn enough to provide adequate food and clothing and recreation;*

The right of every farmer to raise and sell his products at a return which will give him and his family a decent living;

The right of every businessman, large and small, to trade in an atmosphere of freedom from unfair competition and domination by monopolies at home or abroad;

The right of every family to a decent home;

The right to adequate medical care and the opportunity to achieve and enjoy good health;

The right to adequate protection from the economic fears of old age, sickness, accident, and unemployment;

The right to a good education.

All of these rights spell security. And after this war is won we must be prepared to move forward, in the implementation of these rights, to new goals of human happiness and well-being. America's own rightful place in the world depends in large part upon how fully these and similar rights have been carried into practice for our citizens.

For unless there is security here at home there cannot be lasting peace in the world.

One of the great American industrialists of our day—a man who has rendered yeoman service to his country in this crisis-recently emphasized the grave dangers of "rightist reaction" in this Nation. All clear-thinking businessmen share his concern. Indeed, if such reaction should develop—if history were to repeat itself and we were to return to the so-called "normalcy" of the 1920's—then it is certain that even though we shall have conquered our enemies on the battlefields abroad, we shall have yielded to the spirit of Fascism here at home. I ask the Congress to explore the means for implementing this economic bill of rights- for it is definitely the responsibility of the Congress so to do. Many of these problems are already before committees of the Congress in the form of proposed legislation. I shall from time to time communicate with the Congress with respect to these and further proposals. In the event that no adequate program of progress is evolved, I am certain that the Nation will be conscious of the fact.

Our fighting men abroad- and their families at home- expect such a program and have the right to insist upon it. It is to their demands that this Government should pay heed rather than to the whining demands of selfish pressure groups who seek to feather their nests while young Americans are dying. The foreign policy that we have been following—the policy that guided us at Moscow, Cairo, and Teheran—is based on the common sense principle which was best expressed by Benjamin Franklin on July 4, 1776: "We must all hang together, or assuredly we shall all hang separately." I have often said that there are no two fronts for America in this war. There is only one front. There is one line of unity which extends from the hearts of the people at home to the men of our attacking forces in our farthest outposts. When we speak of our total effort, we speak of the factory and the field, and the mine as well as of the battleground -- we speak of the soldier and the civilian, the citizen and his Government. Each and every one of us has a solemn obligation under God to serve this Nation in its most critical hour—to keep this Nation great -- to make this Nation greater in a better world.

The foregoing was the entirety of the text of FDR's 1944 State of the Union Address. The following excerpts are specifically on point to the central theme of this work consider the following:

1. *We are united in determination that this war shall not be followed by another interim which leads to new disaster- that we shall not repeat the tragic errors of ostrich isolationism—that we shall not repeat the excesses of the wild twenties when this Nation went for a joy ride on a roller coaster which ended in a tragic crash.*

2. *The one supreme objective for the future, which we discussed for each Nation individually, and for all the United Nations, can be summed up in one word: Security. And that means not only physical security which provides safety from attacks by aggressors. It means also economic security, social security, moral security—in a family of Nations.*

3. *China and Russia are truly united with Britain and America in recognition of this essential fact: The best interests of each Nation, large and small, demand that all freedom-loving Nations shall join together in a just and durable system of peace. In the present world situation, evidenced by the actions of Germany, Italy, and Japan, unquestioned military control over disturbers of the peace is as necessary among Nations as it is among citizens in a community. And an equally basic essential to peace is a decent standard of living for all individual men and women and children in all Nations. Freedom from fear is eternally linked with freedom from want.*

4. *The overwhelming majority of our people have met the demands of this war with magnificent courage and understanding. They have accepted inconveniences; they have accepted hardships; they have accepted tragic sacrifices. And they are ready and eager to make whatever further contributions are needed to win the war as quickly as possible- if only they are given the chance to know what is*

required of them. However, while the majority goes on about its great work without complaint, a noisy minority maintains an uproar of demands for special favors for special groups. There are pests who swarm through the lobbies of the Congress and the cocktail bars of Washington, representing these special groups as opposed to the basic interests of the Nation as a whole. They have come to look upon the war primarily as a chance to make profits for themselves at the expense of their neighbors- profits in money or in terms of political or social preferment. Such selfish agitation can be highly dangerous in wartime. It creates confusion. It damages morale. It hampers our national effort. It muddies the waters and therefore prolongs the war.

5.   It is our duty now to begin to lay the plans and determine the strategy for the winning of a lasting peace and the establishment of an American standard of living higher than ever before known. We cannot be content, no matter how high that general standard of living may be, if some fraction of our people—whether it be one-third or one-fifth or one-tenth- is ill-fed, ill-clothed, ill housed, and insecure. This Republic had its beginning, and grew to its present strength, under the protection of certain inalienable political rights—among them the right of free speech, free press, free worship, trial by jury, freedom from unreasonable searches and seizures. They were our rights to life and liberty. As our Nation has grown in size and stature, however—as our industrial economy expanded—these political rights proved inadequate to assure us equality in the pursuit of happiness. We have come to a clear realization of the fact that true individual freedom cannot exist without economic security and independence. "Necessitous men are not free men." People who are hungry and out of a job are the stuff of which dictatorships are made. Among these are:

The right to a useful and remunerative job in the industries or shops or farms or mines of the Nation;

The right to earn enough to provide adequate food and clothing and recreation;

The right of every farmer to raise and sell his products at a return which will give him and his family a decent living;

The right of every businessman, large and small, to trade in an atmosphere of freedom from unfair competition and domination by monopolies at home or abroad;

The right of every family to a decent home;

The right to adequate medical care and the opportunity to achieve and enjoy good health;

The right to adequate protection from the economic fears of old age, sickness, accident, and unemployment;

The right to a good education.

All of these rights spell security. And after this war is won we must be prepared to move forward, in the implementation of these rights, to new goals of human happiness and well-being. America's own rightful place in the world depends in large part upon how fully these and similar rights have been carried into practice for our citizens. For unless there is security here at home there cannot be lasting peace in the world.

FDR's address clearly reflects his experiences as President of the United States during both the Great Depression and the War. He clearly sees and points out the links between the reckless policies and indulgences in the United states during the roaring 1920s, the flawed laizze-faire economic ideals of Adam Smith built upon the flawed rationalizations of the philosophies of the Machiavelli and the Social Darwinists. His observation on the ending of World War I, which ultimately, through the conservative economic policies of the 1920s, resulted in economic Depression and another World War, would not be repeated after the end of the Second World War.

His leadership planned to assure security, and properly so through the notion of a *Second Bill of Rights*. As he reasoned, America's rightful place in the world depends upon how fully the rights enumerated in his prospective *Second Bill of Rights* are put into place. Necessitous men and not free man, People who are hungry and out of a job are the stuff out of which Dictators are made.

Summary - The development of this nation after World War II is essentially a counter-example than that for which FDR gave us his blueprint. In a future section of this work, the extreme nature of wealth inequality that continues to worsen as a direct function of this nation abandoning the ideals that FDR provided as guidance for post war America. This again is a compelling case in point of the resilience of the paradoxical and satanic deceptive essence. The resilient move away from the truth and self-sacrificing of team work and interconnectivity which describes the behavior of the majority of Americans, is subverted by the maniacal lust for wealth of those amongst us with the most acute love of money. In a future section on the extreme wealth disparities of 21st century America, we clearly see that the corruption of the US Currency which restricts capital access and creates financial markets to conjure profits through speculation upon the holdings of financial institutions has given rise to this wealth consolidation, which in turn is creating artificial and induced shortages in the production of essential human services, specifically in the realms of housing, education and health care to support the unfolding of FDRs vision of post war America.

I. Corruption of the Monetary Systems of the United States

This section shall demonstrate that the corruption of the monetary system of the United States perpetuates an illegal system of economic inequities which deprive most Americans practical quiet enjoyment of their Constitutional rights. The root of this corruption is an economic system based upon the errant philosophical theories of Machiavelli and the Social Darwinists which are a function of the universal paradox. The ideals of this construct are the polar opposite of the ideals of Locke and Jefferson. The effects of an economic system based upon the errant philosophy of survival of the fittest, with a governmental system based upon natural law, equality and justice, annihilates much of the liberties guaranteed through the Constitution.

First, we will explore the nature of constitutional rights from the lens of FDR, based upon his experiences as President during the Great Depression and World War II. It follows then, that his vision for the post war world likely possess unique clarity and insight.

Second, we will revisit the construct of the universal paradox and construct economic and money system realities upon the Universal model. To reiterate here, that model is one of an infinite singular cohesive field wrapped in paradox or deception.

Third, the essence of money shall be explored along with the mechanics of the current monetary system. It will be demonstrated as clear, the current processes of privately creating money are the root cause of wealth consolidation and furthermore that this current system will serve to not only maintain the status quo of economic inequality it will, unchecked and unadjusted perpetuate it. It shall further negate, from any reasonable or practical standpoint, a society of man based upon the ideals of Locke and Jefferson built upon Natural Law, equality and justice and assure the continuation of a society based upon the ideals of Machiavelli, Adam Smith and the Social Darwinists. As we have demonstrated previously, the current economic system is based upon the ideals of Social Darwinism. This philosophical systems leads only to suffering and disharmony as it proceeds from a false origin. Social Darwinism starts from the flawed notion of temporal scarcity which leads to its logical expansion into economic scarcity. Were it true that time by its nature was scarce and therefore death man's ultimate reality, then the philosophy of the Social Darwinists, that being Survival of the Fittest would produce the highest and best result as it would maximally harmonize with truth. However, the notion of temporal scarcity has been demonstrated here as being false. It follows then that economic resources are likewise not scarce, they exist in harmony and abundance.

Finally, this section will be summarized such that clarity regarding the specific nature of the corruption of the monetary system will be demonstrated and the cause of that corruption is that it proceeds from the errant philosophical justifications of the Social Darwinists and the flawed economic theory of Adam Smith. These philosophical and economic theories are flawed because they originate from the idea of temporal and economic scarcity which has been demonstrated here as false and a disharmony, it therefore shall always trend toward the production of the disharmonious results of war, poverty and crime.

The following excerpt from FDRs 1944 State of the Union Address provides very simple and extraordinarily clear justification for the preserving, protecting and defending of economic liberty as the Cornerstone of post-war America:

> *"This Republic had its beginning, and grew to its present strength, under the protection of certain inalienable political rights—among them the right of free speech, free press, free worship, trial by jury, freedom from unreasonable searches and seizures. They were our rights to life and liberty. As our Nation has grown in size and stature, however—as our industrial economy expanded—these political rights proved inadequate to assure us equality in the pursuit of happiness. We have come to a clear realization of the fact that true individual freedom cannot exist without economic security and independence. "Necessitous men are not free men." People who are hungry and out of a job are the stuff of which dictatorships are made"*

Since the adoption of the United States Constitution in the 18th Century the nature of the society of men, particularly respecting economic systems has changed. As FDR observed that the basic political rights of the United States Constitution, have proved inadequate to assure equality in the pursuit of happiness and that true individual freedom cannot exist without economic security and independence. As such, his post war vision of society included the adoption of the following:

> We have come to a clear realization of the fact that true individual freedom cannot exist without economic security and independence. "Necessitous men are not free men." People who are hungry and out of a job are the stuff of which dictatorships are made. In our day these economic truths have become accepted as self-evident. We have accepted, so to speak, a second Bill of Rights under which a new basis of security and prosperity can be established for all regardless of station, race, or creed.
>
> Among these are:
>
>> The right to a useful and remunerative job in the industries or shops or farms or mines of the Nation;
>>
>> The right to earn enough to provide adequate food and clothing and recreation;

The right of every farmer to raise and sell his products at a return which will give him and his family a decent living;

The right of every businessman, large and small, to trade in an atmosphere of freedom from unfair competition and domination by monopolies at home or abroad;

The right of every family to a decent home;

The right to adequate medical care and the opportunity to achieve and enjoy good health;

The right to adequate protection from the economic fears of old age, sickness, accident, and unemployment;

The right to a good education.

All of these rights spell security. And after this war is won we must be prepared to move forward, in the implementation of these rights, to new goals of human happiness and well-being. America's own rightful place in the world depends in large part upon how fully these and similar rights have been carried into practice for our citizens. For unless there is security here at home there cannot be lasting peace in the world.

This is the blueprint that the construct of American society was to be built upon as envisioned by FDR. His vision was clear, accurate and in harmony with the true interconnected nature of reality. We, all Americans, commit to preserving, protecting and defending these rights amongst one another. It precisely harmonizes with Locke and Jefferson's visions as each in their turn intuitively recognized that harmony in man's society must be constructed upon the truth of Natural Law, equality and justice.

The nature of the corruption of the United States Monetary system is a function of the paradox. It is therefore useful, yet again, to reiterate the construct of the universal paradox.

1.) All is one;

2.) Existence as a series of experiences or interactions requires more than one element;

3.) There is not more than one element

4.) The foregoing are mutually exclusive, yet both are true

5.) It follows therefore that the existence of the universe balances on Paradox

The construct that emerges from this Paradox is that of a barrier, boundary or separating force. Its operations seem something like a semi-permeable membrane that acts to separate the transcendent and universally interconnected *fifth dimension* from the four dimensions of space-time.

To understand why the monetary system is a function of paradox and deception, we must first explore the essence of money. Money is not an element which resides within the four dimensions of space-time. It is at is essence a symbol. It is an idea only and has no physical properties whatever. A physical coin or dollar bill is merely a derivative symbol, it symbolizes the symbol of money. Exchange value is instantaneously created at the moment that a valuable good or service is produced, for which a quantity of money need likewise be created to symbolize this value to facilitate its efficient and equitable exchange for some different item of perceived equivalent exchange value. Money's purpose is to symbolize the relative value of the goods and services produced by one individual so that all of the members of a community can effectively share one another's talents and work product in a manner that is maximally efficient, equitable and just.

The thread of the paradoxical or satanic runs directly through the construct of money. We have demonstrated here that as the universe is a singularity residing outside the bounds of space time, that the universe is not a function of time. Furthermore, due to its paradoxical nature, to facilitate existence, a paradoxical or satanic semi-permeable membrane acts as a boundary between the interconnected infinite fifth dimension and the four dimensions of space-time.

Original Sin was previously demonstrated as a parallel to this paradoxical, satanic or deceptive construct. As the result of Original Sin, man's ability to understand and see through to the true interconnected nature of reality was sealed, metaphorically sealed, with the closing off of Eden guarded by the Cherubim and Sword of Fire.

Money is a symbol which represents the relative value of the creation of an economic resource as a function of a person's work over time. We have herein, repeatedly reinforced the notion that the toil over time nature of the process of creating an economic resource does not by its nature produce a scarce quantity of economic resource, it produces an abundant quantity of resources. This is true precisely because time is not scarce. If we explore the counter example, based upon the false notion of temporal scarcity we must conclude that economic resources as they are a function of toil over time must be scarce thusly. As we have demonstrated here, money is created to symbolize the relative value of work. It follows therefore, that if we falsely posit temporal scarcity this leads to the logical yet inaccurate extension through to economic resource scarcity and finally monetary scarcity.

Built however upon the truth of interconnectivity wrapped in deception as has been repeatedly demonstrated herein, time is not scarce. This foundational truth leads to the accurate and logical extension, proceeding from a truthful originating point, that economic resources are not scarce and therefore there is no scarcity in the money supply.

However, money has a special and unique property. The person who possesses money can exchange it for economic resources. It is only theoretical that the one who possess the funds created a service of value that he exchanged with another party for the currency. As will be demonstrated here, in 21st Century America this is not remotely the case. Consider the following observations regarding the effects that privatizing the management of the money supply will inevitably lead to:

> *"If the American people ever allow private banks to control the issue of their currency, first by inflation, then by deflation, the banks...will deprive the people of all property until their children wake-up homeless on the continent their fathers conquered.... The issuing power should be taken from the banks and restored to the people, to whom it properly belongs." Thomas Jefferson*

> *"History records that the money changers have used every form of abuse, intrigue, deceit, and violent means possible*

to maintain their control over governments by controlling money and its issuance." *James Madison*

"The Government should create, issue, and circulate all the currency and credits needed to satisfy the spending power of the Government and the buying power of consumers. By the adoption of these principles, the taxpayers will be saved immense sums of interest. Money will cease to be master and become the servant of humanity." *-Abraham Lincoln*

"The real truth of the matter is, as you and I know, that a financial element in the large centers has owned the government ever since the days of Andrew Jackson..." *Franklin D. Roosevelt*

"So he [Christ] made a whip out of cords, and drove all from the temple courts, both sheep and cattle; he scattered the coins of the money changers and overturned their tables. To those who sold doves he said, "Get these out of *here! Stop turning my Father's house into a market!" John 2:15-15*

As was stated previously, the purpose of this work is to demonstrate that the consolidation of wealth in the hands of the few is affront to natural law, such that as a result of this reality, many are denied the practical enjoyment of their Natural rights. Further, it is a corruption of the money supply that has facilitated this illegal consolidation. This process as has just been demonstrated is a function of the universal paradoxical and satanic deception, resulting in the false notion of temporal, economic and monetary scarcity.

The process of financial market speculation along with the securitization process causes the conjuring of Currency based upon temporary, or projected profits of enterprises or forecast volatility in the relative prices of commodities. Upon these dynamics a marketplace has been created in which the nation's largest financial institutions speculate with funds placed in their care. This securitization and speculation process allows for the creation of massive sums of nominal value financial instrument contracts, whose trading occurs outside the regulatory arm of the government. The value of these conjured instruments are denominated in currency terms, and therefore can be liquidated in a manner to then create a claim upon the goods and services provided by other members of the society. These conjured securities create distortions in the money supply and through the distortion funds are consolidated in the hands of the individuals who traffic in these markets: i.e. Senior Bankers, Institutional Traders and the Wealthiest Clients of these institutions.

The notional value of derivatives contracts on world books by many estimates exceeds $1 Quadrillion Dollars. Annual Global GDP is $75 Trillion by comparison. These contracts are essentially casino chips conjured by the trading operations of financial institutions and traded generally beyond governmental regulation. Stated alternatively, these contracts exceed the value of all of the economic output for the entire planet for 13 years.

This platform has allowed for the operators in this marketplace to conjure enormous profits upon their portfolios of traded securities. These funds are then held as accumulated wealth which becomes claims upon the goods and services of the remainder of the workers in the economic system.

As we said earlier the essence of money is to facilitate the equitable and efficient exchange of work between people who have the diverse skills and talents needed to produce the broad range of goods and services needed to sustain humanity. Those who amass monetized claims simply by virtue of owning and trading securitized property, enterprises and commodities, consume massive quantities of goods and services and produce nothing. Therefore, the money supply is thusly distorted by attributing value creation and an increase in the money supply solely as a function of ownership and speculation upon the volatility in pricing relative to the ownership of varying types of securities. Consider yet again the observations of Keynes:

> *"Speculators may do no harm as bubbles on a steady stream of enterprise. But the position is serious when enterprise becomes the bubble on a whirlpool of speculation. When the capital development of a country becomes a by-product of the activities of a casino, the job is likely to be ill-done."*
>
> *The General Theory of Employment, Interest and Money*
> 313

Chapter 12

The State of Long-Term Expectation

We must see and call this process precisely what it is COUNTERFIETING. Consider the following from Article 1 Section 8 of the United States Constitution:

> *[The Congress shall have the power] To provide for the Punishment of counterfeiting the Securities and current Coin of the United States.*

The current processes through which securities are created in the United States and speculated upon is creating great instability. It has resulted in a massive redistribution of wealth into the hands of the wealthy. So much so that the basic needs of our economic system to insure the equitable and just enjoyment of constitutional rights has been and continues to be substantially encroached upon. In considering the vison of post war America that FDR had, when we consider his words:

> *"...As our Nation has grown in size and stature, however—as our industrial economy expanded—these political rights proved inadequate to assure us equality in*

314

the pursuit of happiness. We have come to a clear realization of the fact that true individual freedom cannot exist without economic security and independence. "Necessitous men are not free men." People who are hungry and out of a job are the stuff of which dictatorships are made"

"...America's own rightful place in the world depends in large part upon how fully these and similar rights have been carried into practice for our citizens. For unless there is security here at home there cannot be lasting peace in the world."

The underfunding of health care, education and the destabilization of housing markets are directly caused by the corruption of the money supply. This crime of counterfeiting, has resulted in the denial of constitutional rights among many of the nation's citizens.

Summary: As Keynes observed:

"The outstanding faults of the economic society in which we live are its failure to provide for full employment and its

arbitrary and inequitable distribution of wealth and incomes."

As it was true in Keynes era, so is it true today. It is once again seemingly Self-Evident, that massive wealth distribution inequality is fundamentally unjust and is an affront to Natural Law. That under the false philosophical notions of the Social Darwinists and the broken economic theories of Adam Smith, the existing paradigm of wealth inequality is philosophically and economically justified by these premises which proceed from false starting points.

In our day however, we are able to see that natural law, equality and justice, rationalize with the truthful nature of the universe that of a singular cohesive field which transcends space time, wrapped in paradoxical or satanic deception. It is time that these revealed truths become the basis for the reforms needed to align our economic system with the philosophies of Locke and Jefferson. For when it is only our government that is aligned with the precepts of natural law, justice and equality while the economic system remains built upon the false precepts of survival of the fittest and capitalism, the drive to control economic resources will manifest as control of governmental process through the private financing of elections. As the consolidating of wealth through the mere process of owning and speculating upon financial assets arises from activities which affect a Counterfeiting of the currency they are criminal offenses. They are in fact the only criminal offense that has the potential of destroying the Republic. This is so as the wealth that is amassed as a function of this process is then available to effect the election process in such a manner as to assure that the nature of these crimes remains obscure. They are therefore never investigated and corrective measures are never instituted. This is due in great part to the acquisition of control over the Congress of the United States, as it is that branch of the government that is responsible for regulating the currency and assuring that its money supply is not corrupted in precisely the manner in which it has. It has affected an encroachment upon the liberties of the American people that no foreign enemy has ever approach. The people who traffic in this process, and the members of Congress whose complicity they have purchased or whose ignorance they have induced are in the most imperative sense of the word, Treasonous.

Leaving a government of the people by the people and for the people as an empty carcass. For without the practical ability to the equal enjoyment of life, liberty and the pursuit of happiness, the precepts of natural law justice and equality that the government is founded upon does not exist in reality.

J.   Corruption of the Political System of the United States

The purpose of this work is to demonstrate that the true nature of the universe is that of a singular cohesive field, wrapped in paradox or satanic deception. With man's ability to observe the truth of oneness or interconnectivity, he views himself as a fundamentally disconnected essence from the balance of the universe. From this perspective, as we have repeatedly reinforced, man perceives temporal scarcity and that his existence terminates at the end of an interval of time.

This perspective is inaccurate. In the most accurate sense of the word it is sinful. Earlier in this text we had described the results of Einstein's evaluation of the results of quantum experimentation in relation to his theory of special relativity. He and his colleagues in what has become known as the EPR Paradox concluded that quantum mechanics requires that existence is dependent upon a "non-local" hidden variable. It is described as "non-local" not because it is not close by in the traditional sense but rather because it has no location within the four dimensions of space-time. That outside space-time all things maintain a cohesion. Stated alternatively, all things are one.

As was previously mentioned, man is an element of the existential paradox. To reiterate the paradox is:

1.) All is one;

2.) Existence as a series of experiences or interactions requires more than one element;

3.) There is not more than one element

4.) The foregoing are mutually exclusive, yet both are true

5.) It follows therefore that the existence of the universe balances on Paradox

The construct that emerges from this Paradox is that of a barrier, boundary or separating force. Its operations seem something like a semi-permeable membrane that acts to separate the transcendent and universally interconnected *fifth dimension* from the four dimensions of space-time.

As man has had his ability to see and comprehend the true interconnected nature of the universe blinded by the paradoxical or satanic he has built systems, principally economic and governmental systems based upon the false notion of temporal and economic scarcity. Being built upon an inaccurate understanding of interconnected truth the society of man has developed systems in a manner that is at odds with truth. It is disharmonious and therefore continuously produces the disharmonies of war, poverty and crime.

In the wake of the development of the Printing Press, the great thinkers of the Enlightenment of the 17th and 18th Centuries began to pierce through the satanic and paradoxical and see the true nature of interconnected truth. The birth of the notion of governments of the people, by the people and for the people, righteously founded upon the precepts of Natural Law, equality and justice began to emerge.

This however was only a step in constructing a society that is genuinely founded upon these precepts. The philosophies of Machiavelli and the Social Darwinists and the economic theory of Adam Smith are firmly built upon the paradoxical deception of temporal scarcity. Positing temporal scarcity, as economic resources are a function of time, one must also posit economic scarcity. The false notion of economic scarcity leads to the perpetuation of a society that is blind to the true interconnected nature of the universe. Regardless of the theoretical basis of society being founded upon the ideals of John Locke, Thomas Jefferson and James Madison, the ideals of natural law justice and equality, it is largely impotent to set government ideals upon these precepts while economic ideals remain founded upon the deception of temporal, economic and monetary scarcity.

Those amongst us, in the most loyal homage to the Robber Barons, thereby possessed of the most lustful drive for control that money delusionaly produces may use their illegally and immorally accumulated wealth to drive the selection of the peoples' representatives to Congress. These pre-selected candidates represent the interest of their hyper wealth contributors over the people.

The corruption of the process is most critical with the Congress. As was demonstrated in the previous section the inequitable distribution of wealth is perpetuated by the corruption of the money supply. This process of corruption is both a counterfeiting of the currency in violation of the United States Constitution, and

Treason. However as those who are engaged in this process which results in a dilution of the ability of most Americans to practically enjoy their Constitutional rights, have secured the loyalty of the peoples' representatives through the campaign finance paradigm, these crimes remain undiscovered, uninvestigated and unpunished. Without a dismantling of the current campaign finance paradigm the continuing plague upon this nation of economic injustice shall never be corrected and we will continue to live with the disharmonious results of chaos, war, poverty and crime.

There is no reason at all why all costs for election process cannot be provided publically. All aspects of discussing the issues of any particular election can be delivered via the internet and funded 100% with public funds. Instituting new laws to safeguard this process to assure ALL PRIVATE CONTRIBUTION TO CANDIDATES FOR PUBLIC OFFICE ARE CRIMINALIZED.

K.   Conclusion

Throughout this chapter we have reflected upon key events in the United States since its Civil War, through which the stranglehold over the quiet enjoyment of basic constitutional rights has been tightened. At its root the false precept of temporal scarcity has manifest itself in a socio economic construct which ultimately leads to reconsolidation of wealth in the hands of the few which results in the loss of the practical ability of all Americans to enjoy their natural rights within a societal construct of equality and justice.

The Robber Barron generation had effected a fundamental shift in the soul of this nation. They conjured the spirit of Social Darwinism and Machiavelli and then substituted it for the philosophies of Locke, Jefferson and Madison which righteously called for a construct based upon the notion that all men were created equal and endowed by their Creator with certain inalienable right. It is the task of this generation to crush this aberration in the American journey and install new guards for our future security.

References:

Teaching American History Website (n.d). A Southern Christian View of Slavery. Retrieved January 10, 2016 from: http://teachingamericanhistory.org/library/document/a-southern-christian-view-of-slavery/

Teaching American History Website (n.d). Cornerstone Speech. Retrieved: January 14, 2016 from: http://teachingamericanhistory.org/library/document/cornerstone-speech/

Loury, G. (1995). An American Tragedy: The Legacy of Slavery Lingers in Our Cities' Ghettos. *The Brookings Review,* 38-38.

Jaffa, H. (2000). *A new birth of freedom: Abraham Lincoln and the coming of the Civil War.* Lanham, Md.: Rowman & Littlefield.

Meier, M. (1994). Civil War Draft Records: Exemptions and Enrollments. *Prologue Magazine.* Retrieved: January 16, 2016 from http://www.archives.gov/publications/prologue/1994/winter/civil-war-draft-records.html

Zinn, H. (n.d.). *A people's history of the United States: 1492-2001* (New ed.).

Boltz, M. (2014). *The Civil War: "A rich man's battle but a poor man's war"*. The Washington Time December 31, 2014.

Parker, D (1994) *"The Rise and Fall of The Wonderful Wizard of Oz as a "Parable on Populism" JOURNAL OF THE GEORGIA ASSOCIATION OF HISTORIANS*, vol. 15 (1994), pp. 49-63.

Ladenberg, T (2007) "Conservative Policies and Presidents." *Digital History.* Retrieved January 17, 2016 from: http://www.digitalhistory.uh.edu/teachers/lesson_plans/pdfs/unit9_1.pdf

Zimmerman, D.J. (2012). "Senator Harry S Truman and the Truman Committee: Tackling war industry waste and worse." *Defense Media Network.* Retrieved January 19, 2016 from:

http://www.defensemedianetwork.com/stories/senator-harry-s-truman-and-the-truman-committee/

X. The Internet and a new era of Enlightenment and Revolution

A. Parallels between the Printing Press and the Internet

The purpose of this work, to reiterate, is to demonstrate that the true nature of the universe is that of a cohesive singular field residing outside the bounds of space-time, wrapped in paradox. Further, that the nature of man's consciousness is constructed upon this paradox, such that his ability to see and observe the transcendent universal interconnectivity or oneness has been sealed from his mind and vision. Furthermore, it is in the darkness of this inability to observe the genuine interconnectivity of all things that man is born into the sinful or inaccurate notion of the scarcity of time. It has been man's quest over the millennia to discover the true nature of the world in which he dwells. Through the development of his reasoning ability he has continually broadened his understanding of the true workings of the universe. Man develops his deductive reasoning ability through the process of observing phenomena, evaluating information and then discovering or deducing underlying truths.

In the 15th century, the improvements to the Printing Press attributed to Guttenberg caused a fundamental shift in the quantity of information man was able to gain access to and to rapidly share and disseminate the results of his analysis with others through the printed word.

Likewise, in the late 20th and early 21st centuries the internet has caused a new fundamental shift in the quantity of information man is able to gain access to and rapidly share and disseminate the results of this analysis with other through the digitized word.

To provide context to comparatively and quantitatively evaluate the impact that the Printing Press had and the Internet is having on the evolution of governmental and economic systems consider the following:

To quantify the relative impact of the Printing Press on increasing the rate of Information exchange consider the following: While it is obvious that the Printing Press resulted in a tremendous increase in the rate at which information was shared amongst people, how large was that impact? I suspect there are quite a number of methods that could be utilized to attempt to answer that question.

Relative to the impact of the Printing Press, it presents as reasonable to compare the rates of the two different methods of producing reading materials. How many pages could be produced per hour through handwriting vs. the printing press? Guttenberg's Printing Press as it had been improved through the 15th and 16th Centuries could produce approximately 3,600 printed pages per hour while a scribe could produce 3 pages per hour. Using this metric as a barometer it is reasonable to assert that the quantity of information that people were able to access increased over 1,000 fold as a result of the printing press.

Relative to the impact of the Internet, the basis of "information use" presents as a reasonable basis to compare the quantity of information available in the pre and post internet ages that a person could gain ready access to. Prior to the internet, if a person wished to gain knowledge on a given subject, time in the library would be the way to go. During that working session the person would have had access to the quantity of data contained in the volumes of the library. If, for the sake of this analysis we presume the largest of libraries, The Library of Congress, we then would wish to know how many volumes it contains. The Library of Congress contains a total of 110 Million volumes. If we then presume the average volume contains 100,000 words and the average word contains 5 letters, this expands to a total store of data at the largest library in the United States of 55 Trillion bits of information or 55 Terabytes. The entire storage capacity of the internet is currently estimate at 300 Exabytes, or 300 Quintillion bytes. Using this metric as a barometer, it is reasonable to assert that the quantity of information that people are able to access has increased over 5 Million times over as a result of the advent of the internet.

It yet again presents as self-evident that the Enlightenment was influenced and shaped by the printed word. It does not seem a reach to assert that the Enlightenment of the 17th and 18th centuries was indeed a function of the advent of the printing press and that evolution of Enlightenment thought was to a certainty, dependent upon it. For the purpose of this work, the printed word was presumed a pre-requisite to the development of the ideals of John Locke whereby his analysis and reasoning brought him to see the unequivocal truth and righteousness of the precepts of natural law, equality and justice as the proper founding principles for governmental systems. It follows therefore that the political revolution in 17th Century England away from absolute monarchy and the American and French Revolutions of the 18th Centuries were likewise functions of and dependent upon the 1,000 fold increase in information circulation technology that was the Printing Press.

In precisely the same manner, the 5 Million fold increase in information circulation technology that is the internet is fueling a new era of enlightenment. This new era of enlightenment will result in the tearing down of the existing economic paradigm based upon the errant philosophies of Machiavelli and the Social Darwinists and flawed economic theory of Adam Smith in favor of a new economic paradigm which harmonizes with the universal truth of quantum universal connectivity, natural law, equality and justice. This is not a possible outcome it will be the outcome. Only the timing is unknown, how much time will be required? The time interval between the Printing Press and the end of the French Revolution was approximately 360 years (1440 to 1799). The advent of the internet is roughly estimated to be 1995. 20 years have elapsed. These revolutionary economic changes may take up to an additional 2 generations to come to fruition. In any event, the time horizon is certainly no longer that 50 years. Question is how much of this inevitable reform will unfold over the next 20 years? Consider the words of Dr. Martin Luther King:

> *"My dear and abiding friends, Ralph Abernathy, and to all of the distinguished Americans seated here on the rostrum, my friends and co-workers of the state of Alabama, and to all of the freedom-loving people who have assembled here this afternoon from all over our nation and from all over the world: Last Sunday, more than eight thousand of us started on a mighty walk from Selma, Alabama. We have walked through desolate valleys and across the trying hills. We have walked on meandering highways and rested our bodies on rocky byways. Some of our faces are burned from the outpourings of the sweltering sun. Some have literally slept in the mud. We have been drenched by the rains. Our bodies are tired and our feet are somewhat sore. But today as I stand before you and think back over that great*

march, I can say, as Sister Pollard said—a seventy-year-old Negro woman who lived in this community during the bus boycott—and one day, she was asked while walking if she didn't want to ride. And when she answered, "No," the person said, "Well, aren't you tired?" And with her ungrammatical profundity, she said, "My feets is tired, but my soul is rested." And in a real sense this afternoon, we can say that our feet are tired, but our souls are rested. They told us we wouldn't get here. And there were those who said that we would get here only over their dead bodies, but all the world today knows that we are here and we are standing before the forces of power in the state of Alabama saying, "We ain't goin' let nobody turn us around."

Now it is not an accident that one of the great marches of American history should terminate in Montgomery, Alabama. Just ten years ago, in this very city, a new philosophy was born of the Negro struggle. Montgomery was the first city in the South in which the entire Negro community united and squarely faced its age-old *oppressors. Out of this struggle, more than bus desegregation was won; a new idea, more powerful than guns or clubs was born. Negroes took it and carried it across the South in epic battles that electrified the nation and the world. Yet, strangely, the climactic conflicts always were fought and won on Alabama soil. After Montgomery's, heroic confrontations loomed up in Mississippi, Arkansas, Georgia, and elsewhere. But not until the colossus of segregation was challenged in Birmingham did the conscience of America begin to bleed. White America was profoundly aroused by Birmingham because it witnessed the whole community of Negroes facing terror and brutality with majestic scorn and heroic courage. And from the wells of this democratic spirit, the nation finally forced Congress to write legislation in the hope that it would eradicate the stain of Birmingham. The Civil Rights Act of 1964 gave Negroes some part of their rightful dignity, but without the vote it was dignity without strength. Once more the method of nonviolent resistance was unsheathed from its scabbard, and once again an entire community was mobilized to confront the adversary. And again the brutality of a dying order shrieks across the land. Yet, Selma, Alabama, became a shining moment in the conscience of man. If the worst in American life lurked in its dark streets, the best of American instincts arose passionately from across the nation to overcome it. There never was a moment in American history more honorable and more inspiring than the pilgrimage of clergymen and laymen of every race and faith pouring into Selma to face danger at the side of its embattled Negroes. The confrontation of good and evil compressed in the tiny community of Selma generated the massive power to turn the whole nation to a new course. A president born in the South had the sensitivity to feel the will of the country, and in an address that will live in history as one of the most passionate pleas for human rights ever made by a president of our nation, he pledged the might of the federal government to cast off the centuries-old blight. President Johnson rightly praised the courage of the Negro for awakening the conscience of the nation. On our part we must pay our profound respects to the white Americans who cherish their democratic traditions over the ugly customs and privileges of generations and come forth boldly to join hands with us. From Montgomery to Birmingham, from Birmingham to Selma, from Selma back to Montgomery, a trail wound in a circle long and often bloody, yet it has become a highway up from darkness. Alabama has tried to nurture and defend evil, but evil is choking to death in the dusty roads and streets of this state. So I stand before you this afternoon with the conviction that segregation is on its deathbed in Alabama, and the only thing uncertain about it is how costly the segregationists and Wallace will make the funeral. Our whole campaign in Alabama has been centered around the right to vote. In focusing the attention of the nation and the world today on the flagrant denial of the right to vote, we are exposing the very origin, the root cause, of racial segregation in the Southland. Racial segregation as a way of life did not come about as a natural result of hatred between the races immediately after the Civil War. There were no laws segregating the races then. And as the noted historian, C. Vann Woodward, in his book, The Strange*

Career of Jim Crow, clearly points out, the segregation of the races was really a political stratagem employed by the emerging Bourbon interests in the South to keep the southern masses divided and southern labor the cheapest in the land. You see, it was a simple thing to keep the poor white masses working for near-starvation wages in the years that followed the Civil War. Why, if the poor white plantation or mill worker became dissatisfied with his low wages, the plantation or mill owner would merely threaten to fire him and hire former Negro slaves and pay him even less. Thus, the southern wage level was kept almost unbearably low. Toward the end of the Reconstruction era, something very significant happened. That is what was known as the Populist Movement. The leaders of this movement began awakening the poor white masses and the former Negro slaves to the fact that they were being fleeced by the emerging Bourbon interests. Not only that, but they began uniting the Negro and white masses into a voting bloc that threatened to drive the Bourbon interests from the command posts of political power in the South. To meet this threat, the southern aristocracy began immediately to engineer this development of a segregated society. I want you to follow me through here because this is very important to see the roots of racism and the denial of the right to vote. Through their control of mass media, they revised the doctrine of white supremacy. They saturated the thinking of the poor white masses with it, thus clouding their minds to the real issue involved in the Populist Movement. They then directed the placement on the books of the South of laws that made it a crime for Negroes and whites to come together as equals at any level. And that did it. That crippled and eventually destroyed the Populist Movement of the nineteenth century. If it may be said of the slavery era that the white man took the world and gave the Negro Jesus, then it may be said of the Reconstruction era that the southern aristocracy took the world and gave the poor white man Jim Crow. He gave him Jim Crow. And when his wrinkled stomach cried out for the food that his empty pockets could not provide, he ate Jim Crow, a psychological bird that told him that no matter how bad off he was, at least he was a white man, better than the black man. And he ate Jim Crow. And when his undernourished children cried out for the necessities that his low wages could not provide, he showed them the Jim Crow signs on the buses and in the stores, on the streets and in the public buildings. And his children, too, learned to feed upon Jim Crow, their last outpost of psychological oblivion. Thus, the threat of the free exercise of the ballot by the Negro and the white masses alike resulted in the establishment of a segregated society. They segregated southern money from the poor whites; they segregated southern mores from the rich whites; they segregated southern churches from Christianity; they segregated southern minds from honest thinking; and they segregated the Negro from everything. That's what happened when the Negro and white masses of the South threatened to unite and build a great society: a society of justice where none would pray upon the weakness of others; a society of plenty where greed and poverty would be done away; a society of brotherhood where every man would respect the dignity and worth of human personality. We've come a long way since that travesty of justice was perpetrated upon the American mind. James Weldon Johnson put it eloquently. He said:

We have come over a way. That with tears hath been watered.

We have come treading our paths. Through the blood of the slaughtered.

Out of the gloomy past, Till now we stand at last

Where the white gleam Of our bright star is cast.

Today I want to tell the city of Selma, today I want to say to the state of Alabama, today I want to say to the people of America and the nations of the world, that we are not about to turn around. We are on the move now. Yes, we are on the move and no wave of racism can stop us. We are on the move now. The burning of our churches will not deter us. The bombing of our homes will not dissuade us. We are on the move now. The beating and killing of our clergymen and young people will not divert us. We are on the move now. The wanton release of their known murderers would not discourage us. We are on the move now. Like an idea whose time has come, not even the marching of mighty armies can halt us. We are moving to the land of freedom.

Let us therefore continue our triumphant march to the realization of the American dream. Let us march on segregated housing until every ghetto or social and economic depression dissolves, and Negroes and whites live side by side in decent, safe, and sanitary housing. Let us march on segregated schools until every vestige of segregated and inferior education becomes a thing of the past, and Negroes and whites study side-by-side in the socially-healing context of the classroom.

Let us march on poverty until no American parent has to skip a meal so that their children may eat. March on poverty until no starved man walks the streets of our cities and towns in search of jobs that do not exist. Let us march on poverty until wrinkled stomachs in Mississippi are filled, and the idle industries of Appalachia are realized and revitalized, and broken lives in sweltering ghettos are mended and remolded. Let us march on ballot boxes, march on ballot boxes until race-baiters disappear from the political arena. Let us march on ballot boxes until the salient misdeeds of bloodthirsty mobs will be transformed into the calculated good deeds of orderly citizens. Let us march on ballot boxes until the Wallaces of our nation tremble away in silence. Let us march on ballot boxes until we send to our city councils, state legislatures and the United States Congress, men who will not fear to do justly, love mercy, and walk humbly with thy God. Let us march on ballot boxes until brotherhood becomes more than a meaningless word in an opening prayer, but the order of the day on every legislative agenda. Let us march on ballot boxes until all over Alabama God's children will be able to walk the earth in decency and honor. There is nothing wrong with marching in this sense. The Bible tells us that the mighty men of Joshua merely walked about the walled city of Jericho and the barriers to freedom came tumbling down. I like that old Negro spiritual, "Joshua Fit the Battle of Jericho." In its simple, yet colorful, depiction of that great moment in biblical history, it tells us that:

> *Joshua fit the battle of Jericho, Joshua fit the battle of Jericho,*
>
> *And the walls come tumbling down. Up to the walls of Jericho they marched, spear in hand.*
>
> *"Go blow them ramhorns," Joshua cried, "Cause the battle am in my hand."*

These words I have given you just as they were given us by the unknown, long-dead, dark-skinned originator. Some now long-gone black bard bequeathed to posterity these words in ungrammatical form, yet with emphatic pertinence for all of us today. The battle is in our hands. And we can answer with creative nonviolence the call to higher ground to which the new directions of our struggle summons us. The road ahead is not altogether a smooth one. There are no broad highways that lead us easily and inevitably to quick solutions. But we must keep going.

In the glow of the lamplight on my desk a few nights ago,
I gazed again upon the wondrous sign of our times, full
of hope and promise of the future. And I smiled to see in
the newspaper photographs of many a decade ago, the
faces so bright, so solemn, of our valiant heroes, the
people of Montgomery. To this list may be added the
names of all those who have fought and, yes, died in the
nonviolent army of our day: Medgar Evers, three civil
rights workers in Mississippi last summer, William
Moore, as has already been mentioned, the Reverend
James Reeb, Jimmy Lee Jackson, and four little girls in
the church of God in Birmingham on Sunday morning.
But in spite of this, we must go on and be sure that they
did not die in vain. The pattern of their feet as they walked
through Jim Crow barriers in the great stride toward
freedom is the thunder of the marching men of Joshua,
and the world rocks beneath their tread. My people, my
people, listen. The battle is in our hands. The battle is in
our hands in Mississippi and Alabama and all over the
United States. I know there is a cry today in Alabama, we
see it in numerous editorials: "When will Martin Luther

345

King, SCLC, SNCC, and all of these civil rights agitators and all of the white clergymen and labor leaders and students and others get out of our community and let Alabama return to normalcy?" But I have a message that I would like to leave with Alabama this evening. That is exactly what we don't want, and we will not allow it to happen, for we know that it was normalcy in Marion that led to the brutal murder of Jimmy Lee Jackson. It was normalcy in Birmingham that led to the murder on Sunday morning of four beautiful, unoffending, innocent girls. It was normalcy on Highway 80 that led state troopers to use tear gas and horses and billy clubs against unarmed human beings who were simply marching for justice. It was normalcy by a cafe in Selma, Alabama, that led to the brutal beating of Reverend James Reeb.

It is normalcy all over our country which leaves the Negro perishing on a lonely island of poverty in the midst of vast ocean of material prosperity. It is normalcy all over Alabama that prevents the Negro from becoming a registered voter. No, we will not allow Alabama to return to normalcy. The only normalcy that we will settle for is the normalcy that recognizes the dignity and worth of all of God's children. The only normalcy that we will settle for is the normalcy that allows judgment to run down like waters, and righteousness like a mighty stream. The only normalcy that we will settle for is the normalcy of brotherhood, the normalcy of true peace, the normalcy of justice.

And so as we go away this afternoon, let us go away more than ever before committed to this struggle and committed to nonviolence. I must admit to you that there are still some difficult days ahead. We are still in for a season of suffering in many of the black belt counties of Alabama, many areas of Mississippi, many areas of Louisiana. I must admit to you that there are still jail cells waiting for us, and dark and difficult moments. But if we will go on with the faith that nonviolence and its power can transform dark yesterdays into bright tomorrows, we will be able to change all of these conditions. And so I plead with you this afternoon as we go ahead: remain committed to nonviolence. Our aim must never be to defeat or humiliate the white man, but to win his friendship and understanding. We must come to see that the end we seek is a society at peace with itself, a society that can live with its conscience. And that will be a day not of the white man, not of the black man. That will be the day of man as man.

I know you are asking today, "How long will it take?" Somebody's asking, "How long will prejudice blind the visions of men, darken their understanding, and drive bright-eyed wisdom from her sacred throne?" Somebody's asking, "When will wounded justice, lying prostrate on the streets of Selma and Birmingham and communities all over the South, be lifted from this dust of shame to reign supreme among the children of men?" Somebody's asking, "When will the radiant star of hope be plunged against the nocturnal bosom of this lonely night, plucked from weary souls with chains of fear and the manacles of death? How long will justice be crucified, and truth bear it?" I come to say to you this afternoon, however difficult the moment, however frustrating the hour, it will not be long, because "truth crushed to earth will rise again." How long? Not long, because "no lie can live forever." How long? Not long, because "you shall reap what you sow." How long? Not long: Truth forever on the scaffold, Wrong forever on the throne, Yet that scaffold sways the future, And, behind the dim unknown, Standeth God within the shadow, Keeping watch above his own. How long? Not long, because the arc of the moral universe is long, but it bends toward justice. How long? Not long, because: Mine eyes have seen the glory of the coming of the Lord; He is trampling out the vintage where the grapes of wrath are stored; He has loosed the fateful lightning of his terrible swift sword; His truth is marching on. He has sounded forth the trumpet that shall never call retreat; He is sifting out the hearts of men before His judgment seat. O, be swift, my soul, to answer Him! Be jubilant my feet! Our God is marching on. Glory, hallelujah! Glory, hallelujah! Glory, hallelujah! Glory, hallelujah! His truth is marching on.

B. Early 21ˢᵗ Century Wealth Disparity

Without question the best presentation of wealth distribution

inequality is the survey work done by Ariely and Norton. Consider

the following table:

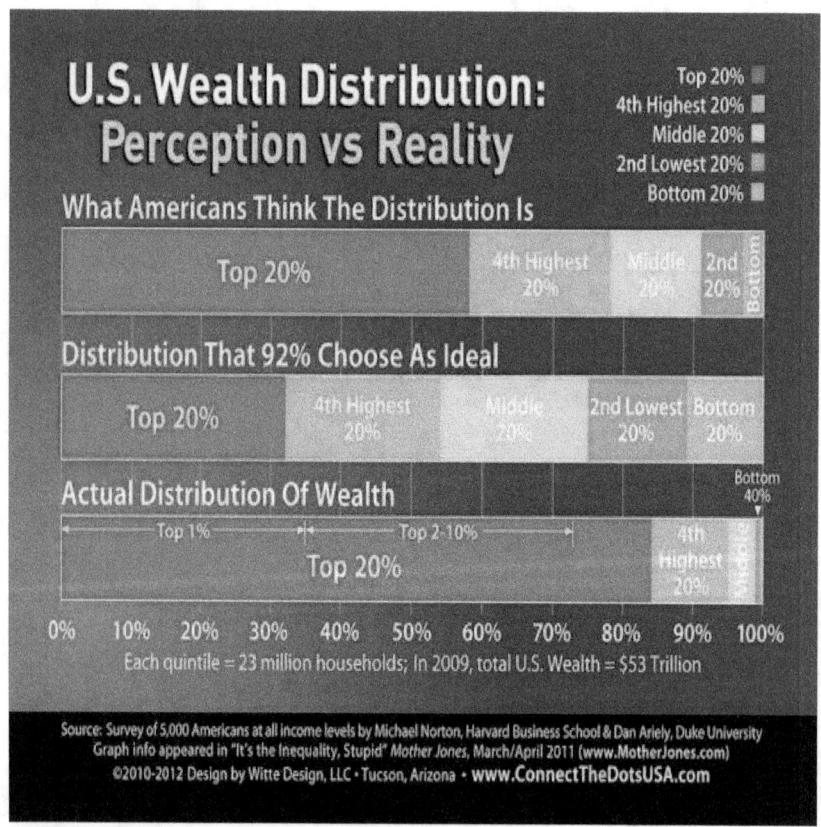

The graph above discloses the following:

- 60% of All American families share approximately 5%

  of the nations' economic resources. This results in 184

  Million Americans living in homes with net worths of

less than $35,000. This level of wealth negates the practical ability of these Americans to secure the resources needed to assure their ability to quietly enjoy their constitutionally guaranteed rights. This again is true specifically as the governmental constructs of natural law, equality and justice are largely impotent as the economic system is based upon the errant philosophies of Machiavelli and the Social Darwinists and the economic theory of Adam Smith. To recall from FDR's 1944 State of the Union Address:

> *"..an equally basic essential to peace is a decent standard of living for all individual men and women and children in all Nations. Freedom from fear is eternally linked with freedom from want."*

> *"We cannot be content, no matter how high that general standard of living may be, if some fraction of our people—whether it be one-third or one-fifth or one-tenth- is ill-fed, ill-clothed, ill housed, and insecure. This Republic had its beginning, and grew to its present strength, under the protection*

of certain inalienable political rights—among them the right of free speech, free press, free worship, trial by jury, freedom from unreasonable searches and seizures. They were our rights to life and liberty. As our Nation has grown in size and stature, however—as our industrial economy expanded—these political rights proved inadequate to assure us equality in the pursuit of happiness. We have come to a clear realization of the fact that true individual freedom cannot exist without economic security and independence. "Necessitous men are not free men." People who are hungry and out of a job are the stuff of which dictatorships are made"

- The above chart discloses that 184 Million Americans in the aggregate own $2.65 Trillion of wealth, while, per the 2015 Forbes Wealth Rankings, the wealthiest 400 American Billionaires own $2.4 Trillion of wealth. As we have previously demonstrated, money is the right to a claim on the services of other. It follows therefore that, 400 Americans control life in the United States to precisely the same extent as 184 Million of us. In no rational manner can this reality equate with the characteristics of a harmonious Republic built upon the notions of natural law, equality and justice, it is practically speaking, of nearly no difference than the feudal system which existed prior to the Enlightenment and the emergence of the notion that governmental systems, to be proper and sustainable must be based upon the principles of natural law, equality and justice. This is not yet the American Reality.

All other economic statistics provide nothing but an obscuring view of the realities of economic security among the people of the United States in the early 21st Century. This richest and most powerful of nations permits a majority of its population to live in a perpetual state of economic insecurity so that the wealthiest of the wealthy, who have learned to traffic in the ownership and speculative trading in financial assets and through the political corruption that is the current campaign finance paradigm, perpetrate these crimes without fear of account. They live in obscene indulgence outside the reach of justice as they have, for a price, acquired the mechanisms of the peoples' justice and in so doing rendered equality an arcane, novel, sentimental and largely fictional notion. Consider:

> *"Now listen, you rich people, weep and wail because of the misery that is coming on you. Your wealth has rotted, and moths have eaten your clothes. Your gold and silver are corroded. Their corrosion will testify against you and eat your flesh like fire. You have hoarded wealth in the last days. Look! The wages you failed to pay the workers who mowed your fields are crying out against you. The cries of the harvesters have reached the ears of the Lord Almighty. You have lived on earth in luxury and self-indulgence. You have fattened yourselves in the day of slaughter. You have condemned and murdered the innocent one, who was not opposing you."* James 5: 1-6

> *"Again I tell you, it is easier for a camel to go through the eye of a needle than for someone who*

is rich to enter the kingdom of God."   *Matthew 19:24*

As was previously observed, a new enlightenment era is unfolding as a function of the instantaneous access to information that is the technology of the internet. This information shall be evaluated and clarity brought to bear to tear down the broken economic and political paradigm which continues to keep a majority of this nation's citizens in perpetual economic insecurity.

C. Break down of Representative Democracy as a function of Monetary System and Political Corruption

The purpose of this work is to demonstrate the foundational truth that the universe is a singular cohesive field which resides outside of the bounds of space-time, wrapped in an existential paradox. This paradox is synonymous with satanic deception. The deception is essential to permit the process of existence which requires a subject and observer to constitute experiences or interactions. As the universe's genuine nature is oneness and interconnectivity deception must lay at the origin of the universe in order for existence to occur.

This deception as has previously been demonstrated here manifests in the mind of man as a false believe in temporal scarcity or death. Sin in its truest and most literal and accurate sense is inaccuracy. Consider once again:

"The wages of Sin is Death" Romans 6:23

To sin in this context is to maintain blindness to the true interconnected construct of the universe, but rather to believe the results of the paradox or satanic deception to be the true nature of reality. It is not. Yet, as man proceeds from this errant originating

356

point in his perspective on truth his ability to observe the trans-dimensional cohesion of reality is obscured, he sees only disconnection and a series of separate elements. From this perspective his personal existence is limited by time. Time is therefore falsely perceived as scarce. To introduce efficiencies and equity into his economic reality the concept of money was developed. Its genuine and useful purpose is to find a commonly accepted means to equitably quantify the relative value a person's work so as to provide a system in which talents can be maximized and the use of those talents can be fairly exchange for the fruits of the broad range of talents needed to harmoniously, equitably and efficiently sustain society.

As has likewise been demonstrated the modern monetary system has been corrupted by activities which result in the distortion of the money supply for the purpose of expanding the wealth of the craftiest and most sinful of individuals. Consider yet again:

> *"For the love of money is the root of many evils" 1 Timothy 6:10*

These activities are direct and clear crimes against the dignity of the American people and the United States Constitution. The current campaign finance paradigm virtually assures that in order to be a viable candidate for the Congress of the United States, funds must be raised from the wealthiest of individuals whose agenda is to maximize the rate at which their accumulated wealth grows and their control over the rights of other Americans results in a greater intrusion by the hyper wealthy into the lives of a majority of the nation's citizens such that the quiet enjoyment of their natural right in an equitable and just manner is denied them. Consider yet again the observations of Keynes:

> *"The outstanding faults of the economic society in which we live are its failure to provide for full employment and its arbitrary and inequitable distribution of wealth and incomes."*

> *The General Theory of Employment, Interest and Money*
>
> *John Maynard Keynes*
>
> *Chapter 24.*
>
> *Concluding Notes on the Social Philosophy towards which the General Theory might Lead*

The society in which we live remains flawed in precisely the same manner as was Keynes. This fault arises directly from man's eyes and mind being blinded to the true oneness of the Universe. This false perception of temporal scarcity results in the false notion of economic scarcity which lays at the heart of the false notion of monetary scarcity. Consider the following observation of Abraham Lincoln:

> *"The Government should create, issue, and circulate all the currency and credits needed to satisfy the spending power of the Government and the buying power of consumers. By the adoption of these principles, the taxpayers will be saved immense sums of interest. Money will cease to be master and become the servant of humanity."*

It is the false perception of the scarcity of money that, to paraphrase the foregoing from Lincoln causes money to master rather than serve society as its regulated quantity is insufficient to satisfy the spending power of the government and the buying power of consumers. Its regulated quantity remains chronically insufficient as the people's representatives to Congress by complicity or ignorance or both, have allowed private interests to distort the money supply in a manner that results in an unsustainable consolidation of wealth. It is unsustainable if we seek a society based upon the precepts of natural law, justice and equality. It works like clockwork if we want a world based upon the errant philosophies of Machiavelli and the Social Darwinists and the flawed economic theory of Adam Smith, which have and will continue to produce disharmony, chaos, war, poverty and crime.

To correct this foundational corruption of the US Congress as a direct function of the iterative cycle of illegal financial market crimes and campaign finance corruption, the existing paradigm must end and be replaced.

The new system's ideals are simple: Criminalize all attempts and instances of money from any individual or entity to any candidate for or elected representative of any governmental agency of the United States. Seize all of the assets of the Republican and Democratic Parties and shut down their operation. And finally, institute an internet based process through which candidates, at no cost, can develop their message to the voting public, over which any necessary or desirable public forum can be facilitated, such as public debate. All costs of this system shall be from public funds and any attempt to influence a candidate through financial contributions or otherwise shall be robustly enforced as the Treason it is.

D. Conclusion

The purpose of this chapter has been to demonstrate that the Internet, as a parallel to the Printing Press has affected a quantum shift in the pace at which human enlightenment is maturing. The increased rate at which information and ideas were circulated pre and post Printing Press was demonstrated here as a 1,000 fold increase. The rate of information circulation as a result of the Internet that was demonstrated here was an increase of 5 Million times over.

In the wake of the Printing Press man was able to rationalize the righteousness of natural law, equality and justice as the only desirable and sustainable basis for governmental forms. It follows then that the revolutions of the 17th and 18th centuries away from monarchies to governments of the people by the people and for the people, predicated upon the rationalized notions of natural law, equality and justice resulted. Likewise, the ability to observe transcendent realities, and rationalize through the paradox in the wake of the findings of quantum mechanics of the 1920s, as a function of access to information that is now available through the internet, is giving rise to a new birth of enlightenment. The ability to see through the universal paradox and satanic deception is providing a path over which man can reflect upon the realities of life in the 21st century. The governmental reforms of the 17th and 18th centuries which order these systems upon the natural law precepts of Locke and Jefferson are of practically no effect as economic systems are not yet ordered upon these principles. Modern economic systems remain ordered upon the errant philosophies of Machiavelli and the Social Darwinists and the economic theory of Adam Smith. This ordering is founded upon the falsehood of scarcity. Positing temporal scarcity this extends to both economic and monetary scarcity. Upon this foundation systems consistently move toward corruption which ultimately results in wealth consolidation which negates the practical enjoyment of natural rights by vast portions of society.

The corruption of financial markets are crimes, the crime of counterfeiting. This gravest of crimes has placed the practical survival of the Republic in jeopardy as wealth that is accumulated thusly engages in the process of influencing election process in a manner which assures that these crimes are not investigated nor punished and are in fact left to be committed with no fear whatever of being held to account, as the Congress, the peoples'

representatives, represent the interest of these same criminals for

a price and subordinate their duty to the people thusly.

References:

Human factors guidelines and methodology in the design of a user-computer interface: A case study. (1988). *Applied Ergonomics, 19*(2), 159-160.

XI. Strategic Plan for the Victorious Revolution

A. Second Bill of Rights: Philosophical Foundation for the New Construct

The purpose of this work has been to demonstrate that the genuine and truthful nature of the universe is that of a cohesive singular field residing "Non-locally" outside the four dimensions of space-time wrapped or obscured by paradox or satanic deception.

The following once again, sets forth the nature of the universal paradox:

1.) All is one;

2.) Existence as a series of experiences or interactions requires more than one element;

3.) There is not more than one element;

4.) The foregoing are mutually exclusive, yet both are true;

5.) It follows therefore that the existence of the universe balances on Paradox

As a result of this paradox, man's perspective upon reality is built upon the false or sinful notion of disconnection or separation. Proceeding from this inaccurate or sinful perspective, man has constructed societal, governmental and economic forms built upon this errant foundation. As a result of the expansion of human awareness and reasoning capability that resulted from the increase in information sharing capacity that the Printing Press facilitated staring in the 15th Century, man began to see through to genuine truth during the Enlightenment period. Thus resulting in the movement away from absolute monarchies to governmental forms built upon the precepts of natural law, equality and justice, those ideals which truthfully harmonize with the Universal truth of interconnectivity.

Since the adoption of the notion of governments of the people by the people and for the people built upon the precepts of natural law, equality and justice, society in general has moved very slowly towards this model as economic systems have remained built upon the errant philosophies of Machiavelli and the Social Darwinists and the economic theory of Adam Smith. At their foundation, theses errant ideals are firmly rooted upon the lie of temporal scarcity which then manifests as the notions of economic and monetary scarcity.

Upon this construct, we validated the extreme nature of the realities of wealth distribution inequities in the United States in the Early 21st Century. It was demonstrated that 60% of American household live in essential poverty as their household net worths are insufficient to secure those basic necessities of life need to practically enjoy ones constitutionally guaranteed rights. As FDR rightly observed *"Necessitous men are not free men"*. Further, that it was a criminal cycle of financial markets securitization and speculation that affects a counterfeiting of the currency which gives rise to and perpetuates this wealth distribution paradigm. Further, that this criminal construct is maintained in an iterative manner through the political corruption such that the agency charged with the investigation and punishment of this type of crime, the Congress of the United States, is populated by representatives whose loyalty has been secured by the very people engaging in this abuse. The loyalty of the Congress has been secured by these criminals rendering the Congress incapable of discharging their duty to the American people, this process is of course Treasonous.

To replace the old realities, and as Jefferson emboldened us to do:

"That whenever any Form of Government becomes destructive of these ends, it is the Right of the People to alter or to abolish it, and to institute new Government, laying its foundation on such principles and organizing its powers in such form, as to them shall seem most likely to effect their Safety and Happiness. Prudence, indeed, will dictate that Governments long established should not be changed for light and transient causes; and accordingly all experience hath shewn, that mankind are more disposed to suffer, while evils are sufferable, than to right themselves by abolishing the forms to which they are accustomed. But when a long train of abuses and usurpations, pursuing invariably the same Object evinces a design to reduce them under absolute Despotism, it is their right, it is their duty, to throw off such Government, and to provide new Guards for their future security."

We are fortunate to have a blue print for the new system, it is the set of rights enumerated by FDR in his 1944 State of the Union

Address, they continue to form a foundation upon which, as FDR observed would:

> *"All of these rights spell security. And after this war is won we must be prepared to move forward, in the implementation of these rights, to new goals of human happiness and well-being. America's own rightful place in the world depends in large part upon how fully these and similar rights have been carried into practice for our citizens. For unless there is security here at home there cannot be lasting peace in the world."*

The following sets forth these enumerated rights:

1.) *The right to a useful and remunerative job in the industries or shops or farms or mines of the Nation;*

2.) *The right to earn enough to provide adequate food and clothing and recreation;*

3.) *The right of every farmer to raise and sell his products at a return which will give him and his family a decent living;*

4.) *The right of every businessman, large and small, to trade in an atmosphere of freedom from unfair competition and domination by monopolies at home or abroad;*

5.) *The right of every family to a decent home;*

6.) *The right to adequate medical care and the opportunity to achieve and enjoy good health;*

7.) *The right to adequate protection from the economic fears of old age, sickness, accident, and unemployment;*

8.) *The right to a good education*

These rights will be instituted in the United States. The only question is when. As Dr. Martin Luther King observed regarding the death of segregation in Alabama in 1965, that it was not a question of if but only of when. That the only uncertainty was how expensive men with values like those of then Governor Wallace would cause Segregation's funeral to be. We renew Dr. King's observations here. Economic justice is the destiny of this nation. How expensive and painful a process will it be? How much resistance to righteous and inevitable adjustment to the old paradigm will our hyper-wealthy overlords and the Congress they have purchased via generous campaign contributions present? How much longer shall they seek to hide behind the flawed and dark philosophies of Machiavelli and the Social Darwinists that have been rolled out time and time again to justify great atrocities such as slavery, imperialism the Confederacy's War of Aggression and Oppression, and the modern dynamic of illegally consolidated wealth?

B. Restructure Departments of the Executive to achieve Objective of guaranteeing universal enjoyment of Second Bill of Rights

The central notion of this reform is the instituting of new practices which change the nature of the relationship of families with the larger community of all American families. The two essential elements in the new construct, as economic units, are therefore the family and the Federal Government.

The principal interface is required between these organizations as the family is the cohesive economic unit of our society and it is the federal government through which monetary policies and systems are effectuated.

The current fiscal/monetary paradigm is flawed and is not retrievable. The model of what can work was, from a value standpoint, given to us by Lincoln:

> *"The Government should create, issue, and circulate all the currency and credits needed to satisfy the spending power of the Government and the buying power of consumers. By the adoption of these principles, the taxpayers will be saved immense sums of interest. Money*

will cease to be master and become the servant of humanity."

As has been demonstrated here, scarcity is the flawed assumption that the economic system is built upon. The regulation of the quantity of money within the current system is regressive, it utilizes previously completed economic output as the basis of the money supply. For reasons in part having to do with market abuses but to a greater extent to decouple the money supply from the false notion of scarcity, money shall be issued by the federal government in precisely the quantity necessary, as Lincoln observed, to satisfy the spending power of the Government and the buying power of consumers. We shall make money, in this manner the rightful servant of mankind and no longer its master.

Upon this construct, all forms of tax shall be eliminated. Managing the money supply thusly eliminates the need for taxes. From the perspective of an abundant as opposed to a scarce supply of money no artificially opposed restriction on the production of and circulation of economic resources shall be imposed upon the system. Further, taxation has and always will serve to separate and divide the people of a nation it is not a required element of the emerging quantum economy.

The hyperinflation which occurred in previous systems as the result of coining money for which no goods or services were produced, is precisely to opposite of the new system. In the new, currency shall be provided as need as service and goods are produced in accordance with strategic resource planning. These strategic and subsidiary tactical plans will be designed with a singular objective: to assure all American families have access by right to all resources needed to live in a practical and not only theoretical manner consistent with the promises of the Second Bill of Rights.

The two central agencies of the government which will be necessary for this paradigm are the Treasury and a to-be-formed department whose role is that of family advocacy. Every one of the approximate 110 Million families in the United States shall be assigned a counselor whose role it is to assure that all of the elements of the Second Bill of Rights are accessible by their client families and further still that all individuals are responsibly and held accountable for shouldering their fair share of work based upon long term family planning targets developed collaboratively between the counselor and heads of the households.

The specific resources needed to actualize the enjoyment of the enumerated rights shall likewise be formed. Housing, Education, Health Care, Insurance, Financial Services, Employment Services and Retirement shall likewise be departmentalized in a manner such that Family Counselors facilitate these goods and services on behalf of their client families.

This construct harmonizes with the truth of the abundance of all resources.

C.   Conclusion

To review one final time, the purpose of this work was to demonstrate that the universe is constructed as a singular cohesive field outside the four dimensions of space-time wrapped in paradoxical or satanic deception. The structure of the paradox is as follows:

1.) All is one;

2.) Existence as a series of experiences or interactions requires more than one element;

3.) There is not more than one element;

4.) The foregoing are mutually exclusive, yet both are true;

5.) It follows therefore that the existence of the universe balances on Paradox

That as a function of this universal construct man's consciousness is likewise constructed upon paradoxical or satanic deception. Over the millennia his understanding of reality has expanded. However, rooted in deception he has traveled through the valley of the shadow of death in a manner where he has constructed governmental, social and economic systems based upon his false perception of the scarcity of time.

The printing press and internet provided quantum leaps in the rate at which men could circulate and develop new ideas and deeper understandings of truth. In the wake of the printing press men began establishing governmental systems based upon this newly found ability to rationalize the truthfulness of the equality of all men which harmonizes with universal truth. This advance has had limited benefits as economic systems were not likewise reoriented in this fashion. The continuation of the paradoxical and satanic was continually justified upon the flawed philosophical systems of Machiavelli and the Social Darwinists and errant economic theory of Adam Smith.

The discovery of the mechanisms of quantum physics of the 1920s and 1930s provided a clear validation of the interconnected nature of the universe and its paradoxical construct. It is the duty of this generation to rationalize this paradox and construct new economic systems which result in a society that is practically based upon the righteous philosophies of natural law, justice and equality, in the tradition of Locke and Jefferson.

The current economic paradigm as evidenced by the unsustainable level of wealth disparity is a system which is an affront to natural law, equality and justice. Through the corruption of the existing monetary systems, perpetuated by the corruption of the political system through the current campaign finance paradigm, the existing construct assures that the affront to natural law that is inequitable wealth distribution shall continue in perpetuity.

The existing systems must be replaced and not reformed. As was demonstrated herein time is not scarce. There is therefore no economic nor monetary scarcity. Based upon this righteous perspective of the harmonious abundance of economic resources the new system shall emerge through a reorientation of the manner in which the monetary system is regulated. It shall be regulated based upon the execution of resource specific strategic plans that are developed and orchestrated to assure that all American families have practical access to all of the resources needed to enjoy their fundamental human and natural rights as those rights are enumerated in the Second Bill of Rights framed by FDR in his 1944 State of the Union Address.

Once again, as Jefferson instructed us:

"That whenever any Form of Government becomes destructive of these ends, it is the Right of the People to alter or to abolish it, and to institute new Government, laying its foundation on such principles and organizing its powers in such form, as to them shall seem most likely to effect their Safety and Happiness. Prudence, indeed, will dictate that Governments long established should not be changed for light and transient causes; and accordingly all experience hath shewn, that mankind are more disposed to suffer, while evils are sufferable, than to right themselves by abolishing the forms to which they are accustomed. But when a long train of abuses and usurpations, pursuing invariably the same Object evinces a design to reduce them under absolute Despotism, it is their right, it is their duty, to throw off such Government, and to provide new Guards for their future security."

The demonstrated realities of wealth distribution inequities are a continuing, long train of usurpations and abuses. It is the duty of this generation to rationalize through paradoxical and satanic deception, grab firm hold of the true interconnected nature of the universal construct and by extension the brotherhood of man and institute systems which achieve greater standards of liberty, justice and happiness for all men.

www.ingramcontent.com/pod-product-compliance
Lightning Source LLC
Chambersburg PA
CBHW062122280526
45788CB00001B/22